# WORLD WAR II

# WORLD

US TROOPS PARADING THROUGH PARIS, FRANCE, IN 1944

# WAR II

## SEAN CALLERY

SCHOLASTIC discover more™

# WWII Heroes and Heroines

Download your free digital book and explore the extraordinary lives of war heroes and heroines. Meet code-crackers, courageous soldiers and medics on the battlefield, and children caught up in a war-torn world.

**Your digital book is very simple to use. Enter the code (bottom right) to download it to any Mac or PC. Open it in Adobe Reader, also free to download. Then you're all set!**

## Child heroes

All children in war-torn countries endured hardships, from lack of food to limited clothing and toys. In Europe, thousands of city children were evacuated – sent away to live with strangers in safer areas, sometimes even in different countries. Many children lost parents who died in battle. Many more lost their homes in bombing raids or became **refugees**. Sadly, countless children died, including more than a million children killed by the Nazis and their allies during the Holocaust.

**Goodbye, Daddy**
Many children threw
to face life without
their parents served
Sometimes their pa

### About
# 1.5 million
**Jewish children were killed by Nazis and their collaborators**

A group of children awaiting **evacuation** from London, in autumn 1939 say goodbye to their parents before boarding a train. They travelled far from home to stay with families who took care of them during the war. Some children stayed with their new families for the entire war. Others were very homesick and came back to face life in the **blitz**.

**Evacuees** had a small list of possessions they could take with them, including a change of clothes and a parcel of food.

**A luggage label** tied to each child notified the new carer of the child's name and age.

👁 **Eyewitness account from an evacuee**

🎥 **See inside Anne Frank's hideout**

◉ **discover more**—Anne Frank

# WORLD W
## Heroes and Heroines

**A digital companion to World War**

## Hyperlinks

All of the pages in the digital book are hyperlinked. Click the coloured buttons for more facts and pictures, video clips, personal accounts, and tips for using your digital book.

## Death-defying deeds

Find out what it was like to live through an air raid, go undercover in enemy territory as a secret agent, and meet the people who risked their lives to save others.

# "In spite of everything I still believe that people are really good at heart." —ANNE FRANK

**Consultant:** Terry Charman, Senior Historian, Imperial War Museum London
**Project Editor:** Clare Hibbert
**Project Art Editor:** Mark Lloyd
**Designers:** Clare Joyce, Silke Spingies
**Art Director:** Bryn Walls
**Managing Editor:** Miranda Smith
**Managing Production Editor:** Stephanie Engel
**Cover Designer:** Neal Cobourne
**DTP:** Sunita Gahir, John Goldsmid
**Digital Photography Editor:** Stephen Chin
**Visual Content Project Manager:** Diane Allford-Trotman
**Executive Director of Photography, Scholastic:** Steve Diamond

Library of Congress Cataloging-in-Publication Data Available
Distributed in the UK by Scholastic UK Ltd, Westfield Road, Southam, Warwickshire, England CV47 0RA

ISBN 978-1-407-13652-3

10 9 8 7 6 5 4 3 2     13 14 15 16 17

Printed in Singapore   46
First published 2013

Scholastic is constantly working to lessen the environmental impact of our manufacturing processes. To view our industry-leading paper procurement policy, visit www.scholastic.com/paperpolicy.

" **There is no blinking at the fact that our people, our territory, and our interests are in grave danger** "
—FRANKLIN D. ROOSEVELT, 8 DECEMBER 1941

WOMAN WORKING ON A VENGEANCE DIVE-BOMBER, TENNESSEE, 1943

# Contents

## A show of strength

By 1944, the German army had installed a string of enormous guns, like this one, along the Atlantic coast of France. They were put there to defend the territory that Germany had captured across Europe. By then, the most terrible war in history had also seen conflict in Africa, Asia, and the Pacific. Countries fought to protect the freedom of their people, lands, and ideas.

## Destroyed cities

In World War II, families and children suffered as never before. Hundreds of cities and towns were turned to rubble as battles were fought in, around, and above them. This picture was taken in Saint-Lô, northern France, in July 1944. The scene was similar in Stalingrad in the Soviet Union, Warsaw in Poland, and Dresden in Germany.

# The tov

* What spectacle took place in Berlin in 1936?

* Who led Germany – and the world – into war?

* What was life like for wartime refugees?

path
war

# Road to war [From 1918 to

In the 1930s, militaristic regimes ruled in Germany, Italy, and Japan. Their citizens wanted strong leaders to solve economic problems arising from a worldwide slump and, in Germany, hard conditions imposed by the peace treaties following World War I.

## JAN. 1933
## Adolf Hitler

Hitler, leader of the Nazi Party, took power from President Paul von Hindenburg. Hitler was popular because he promised to make Germany great again. He immediately began to build up the country's army and weapons.

HITLER WITH HINDENBURG

## JULY 1914–NOV. 1918
## WWI

This appalling conflict in which 15 million died was a victory for Britain, France, Russia, and Italy over the German and Austro-Hungarian empires. The victors used the Treaty of Versailles to force Germany to disarm, give up lands, and pay vast sums of money.

ALLIED SOLDIERS FIGHTING IN THE TRENCHES

### SEPT. 1931
*Japan invaded Manchuria, on the east coast of China, to gain vital territory and minerals.*

### AUG. 1936
*Hitler introduced military conscription – against the terms of the Treaty of Versailles, which had limited his army to 100,000 troops.*

•1920•   •1930•

*Dots represent yearly increases until 1939.*

### OCT. 1922
*In Italy, Benito Mussolini, leader of the National Fascist Party, marched on Rome and seized power.*

### JAN. 1924
*In the Communist Soviet Union (now Russia), Vladimir Lenin died. Joseph Stalin took control.*

### OCT. 1935
*Eager to gain territory in Africa, Italy used powerful mustard gas to help it conquer Abyssinia (now Ethiopia).*

### MAR. 1936
*When German troops entered the Rhineland, on the border with France, no one tried to stop them.*

## OCT. 1929
## The crash

The collapse of the New York Stock Exchange on Wall Street triggered the Great Depression, an economic slump that spread across the Western world. Millions lost their jobs and savings, and Germany suffered badly.

CROWDS PANICKING ON WALL STREET

## JULY 1936
## Trouble in Spain

When the Spanish Civil War began, Hitler and Mussolini helped the nationalist general Francisco Franco to victory. The German air force carried out the first large-scale bombings of civilians and destroyed the Spanish town of Guernica in 1937.

### FRANCISCO FRANCO
#### Dictator, Spain

| | |
|---|---|
| In power: | 1936–75 |
| Party: | Nationalist |

## AUG. 1938
# The Spitfire enters service
Britain began building large numbers of this speedy, single-seater fighter plane. War was clearly coming, and control of the skies would be vital to defend the island nation from attack.

PRIDE OF THE RAF: THE SPITFIRE

## 9 NOV. 1938
# Kristallnacht
The Nazi regime brutally oppressed political opponents and minorities, particularly the Jewish people. Kristallnacht ("Crystal Night") is named for all the shattered glass left on German streets after a night destroying Jewish property.

CLEANING UP AFTER KRISTALLNACHT

## MAR. 1938
*Hitler took over the neighbouring nation of Austria. Again, no one challenged him.*

## JULY 1937
*Japan used conquered Manchuria as a base for its ruthless invasion of China.*

## APR. 1939
*Italy invaded Albania. Mussolini was copying Hitler's aggressive empire-building strategy.*

## SEPT. 1939
*France, Britain, and the Commonwealth countries Australia, New Zealand, South Africa, and Canada declared war on Germany. The USA stayed neutral.*

**1939**

## NOV. 1936
*Germany and Italy signed a treaty of friendship, known as the Rome-Berlin Axis.*

*Dots represent monthly increases during 1939.*

## FEB. 1939
*Germany launched a massive battleship, the Bismarck, displaying to the world the power of its navy.*

## AUG. 1939
# German-Soviet Pact
Germany and the Soviet Union agreed not to attack each other, and secretly divided Eastern Europe between them. Germany broke the terms of the Munich Pact and invaded Poland on 1 September.

GERMAN TANKS IN POLAND

### NEVILLE CHAMBERLAIN
**Prime minister, Britain**

| | |
|---|---|
| In power: | 1937–40 |
| Party: | Conservative |

## SEPT. 1938
# Munich Pact
Eager to avoid a war and to support an enemy of Communism, European leaders allowed Hitler to occupy part of Czechoslovakia. The British prime minister, Neville Chamberlain, called the deal "peace for our time".

# 38 million:
## the number of gas masks given out in Britain a year after the Munich Pact

The Treaty of Versailles (1919) saw the victors of World War I strip Germany of land and demand huge payments as punishment. This damaged the German economy, and unemployment rose. Adolf Hitler offered an answer, promising to create a new German empire.

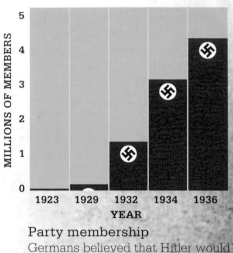

Party membership
Germans believed that Hitler would make their country great again. When the Nazi Party gained power, it controlled who received the best jobs. To gain government employment, one had to join the party. Those who didn't became outsiders.

## Bid for power

Hitler's National Socialist Party, often called the Nazi Party, tried to seize power in 1923. Hitler was found guilty of treason and spent eight months in jail. There he wrote *Mein Kampf* ("*My Struggle*") and outlined his belief that Germany must seize new lands.

Military beginnings
Born in 1889 in a German-speaking part of Austria, Hitler hoped to be an artist. But he always admired Germany and eagerly signed up to fight on its side in World War I (1914–18).

Play money
When the German reichsmark currency collapsed, children played with stacks of banknotes that had no value.

## Worthless money

In 1923, the German monetary system fell apart. The United States aided its recovery with enormous loans. But in 1929, the US economy collapsed with the Wall Street Crash. The US government was forced to call in all of its loans. The resulting worldwide Great Depression hit Germany especially hard.

### Nazi Germany: Timeline

**Sept. 1919** *The army sent Hitler, now a corporal, to spy on extremist groups. He joined the German Workers' Party, forerunner of the Nazi Party.*

**29 July 1921** *Hitler became the Nazi leader and took the title "Führer". His rousing speeches attracted large crowds.*

**9 Nov. 1923** *Hitler failed in an attempt to overthrow the government. At his trial, his speeches received a great deal of publicity.*

**4 Apr. 1925** *The Schutzstaffel (SS) was formed. It was led by Heinrich Himmler, who later ran the Gestapo, or secret police.*

## Hitler takes over

In January 1933, after an election with no clear winner, German president Paul von Hindenburg appointed Hitler chancellor, leading a multi-party government.

But Hitler used emergency powers to take over running the state. When Hindenburg died in August 1934, Hitler became president.

**Hitler Youth**
German children had to join a Nazi youth organization. They were taught to love Germany and hate Jews and Communists.

## The Third Reich

Hitler created jobs by strengthening the army and starting new building projects. He wanted to establish an empire known as the Third Reich (*Reich* means "empire"). The previous ones had been the Holy Roman Empire (800–1806) and the German Empire (1871–1918).

**Technology**
Hitler funded research on new military technologies. Scientist Wernher von Braun's work in the 1930s led to a pioneering rocket missile, the V-2.

**Flag for the new empire**
The German flag was black, red, and yellow. In 1935, a new flag combined the red, white, and black colours of the Second Reich, plus the Nazi swastika (see page 20).

**Transport**
Hitler ordered the design of a Volkswagen ("people's car") – an affordable car for German families. The first ones were rolled out in 1938.

**Jan. 1929** *Joseph Goebbels took charge of Nazi propaganda. He used radio, films, newspapers, and rallies to spread the Nazi message.*

**5 Mar. 1933** *The Nazis won 44 percent of votes in a general election. Hitler continued to eliminate all opposition and centralize power.*

**15 Sept. 1935** *Hitler passed new laws that made Jews second-class citizens. They no longer had the right to vote in elections.*

**7 Mar. 1936** *Hitler started reclaiming land for the Reich. He put troops in the Rhineland for the first time since World War I.*

# The Berlin Olympics [Nazi

The 1936 Summer Olympics were held in Berlin, the capital of Germany. Nazi dictator Hitler used them to showcase the military efficiency of his nation. The 49 competing countries did not challenge Hitler then or in the years that followed, even when he invaded neighbouring countries. No one wanted to provoke a war.

## Jesse Owens

The hero of the Games was African American athlete Jesse Owens, who won 4 gold medals and broke 11 Olympic records. His triumphs included defeating German star athlete Lutz Long in the long jump. Hitler was furious that an "inferior" person had defeated a white person.

On the podium
At the medal ceremony, Long (right) gave a Nazi salute during the playing of the US national anthem.

## Appeasing Hitler

The major European powers were worn out by war. Many thought that the reparations imposed on Germany in 1919 were harsh and that, like them, Hitler opposed Communism. They allowed Germany to invade Austria and, in late 1938, signed the Munich Pact.

Munich accord
Hitler and British prime minister Neville Chamberlain shake hands in Munich, 1938.

## Czech invasion

The Munich Pact allowed Hitler to take over part of Czechoslovakia. The conquest of the rest of the country then became Hitler's goal. In 1939, German troops marched over the border. The other European powers suddenly realized that they could no longer trust Hitler.

Conquered city
The name of the Square of Liberty in the Czech city of Brno is changed to Adolf Hitler Square.

## Nazi Germany: Time line

**7 Mar. 1936** *More than 32,000 German soldiers marched into the Rhineland, bordering France. They met no opposition.*

**25 Nov. 1936** *Germany and Japan signed the Anti-Comintern Pact against the Communist Soviet Union. Italy joined in 1937.*

**12 Mar. 1938** *Hitler entered Vienna, Austria, breaking the Treaty of Versailles. The other western powers took no action.*

**29 Sept. 1938** *Hitler promised not to invade other lands if he was given part of Czechoslovakia in the Munich Pact.*

# showcase]

## One month

before the Games, top German high jumper Gretel Bergmann was dropped for being Jewish

### Crowd-pleaser
Hitler used the Berlin Games to gain popularity in Germany and to promote his image around the world. Huge crowds showed their support with salutes and chants of *"Sieg Heil"* ("Hail to victory").

**16 Mar. 1939** *Germany occupied the rest of Czechoslovakia. Again, other western powers did nothing to stop Hitler.*

**Aug. 1939** *Germany and the Soviet Union signed a non-aggression pact. They agreed to share Poland between them.*

**1 Sept. 1939** *Assured of Italy's support, Germany invaded Poland. Britain and France responded by declaring war on Germany.*

## More here
*For key to symbols, see page 112*

**1936 Berlin Olympics**
**Nazi  Hitler  Jesse Owens**
**Anti-Comintern Pact**
Czechoslovakia

*The Nazi Olympics:*
*Berlin 1936*
by Susan D. Bachrach

*Flying a Flag for*
*Hitler: My Childhood*
*in Nazi Germany*
by Elsbeth Emmerich

*Good-Bye Marianne:*
*A Story of Growing Up*
*in Nazi Germany*
by Irene N. Watts

Leni Riefenstahl's *Olympia* documents the 1936 Games; her *Triumph of the Will* shows Hitler's famous rally at Nuremberg in 1934.

Visit the **Olympic Stadium** in Berlin, Germany, now the home of football team Hertha BSC. It is also used for music and other sporting events.

**appeasement:** the act of making undue concessions to satisfy the demands of someone greedy for power.

**Nazi:** a member of Hitler's National Socialist Party in Germany, which promoted racist, authoritarian ideas.

# Ideologies [Big ideas]

During the 1930s, a number of very different (and sometimes opposing) ideologies, or belief systems, were developed around the world. These differences eventually led to war.

**FASCES**

## Fascism

Fascism is named after the fasces, an ancient Roman symbol of authority and power. Fascists value leadership and expect a dictator, or powerful ruler, to tell the people what to do.

**Key points**

| | |
|---|---|
| *Origins:* | Fascist ideas spread from France in the 1880s |
| *Children were taught:* | The state is best |
| *Led by:* | A dictator, so that there are no disputes |
| *Most influential group:* | The military, to protect the state and suppress opposition |
| *Opposed to:* | Communism |

Fascist Italy

### Italy and Benito Mussolini
In 1922, Mussolini and his followers, the Blackshirts, marched on Rome to take power. He became dictator in 1927.

**BENITO MUSSOLINI**

| | |
|---|---|
| *Lived:* | 29 July 1883– 28 April 1945 |
| *Led:* | Italy (1922–45) |
| *Nickname:* | Il Duce ("the Leader") |

## "The people do not know what they want. . . . I have stopped the talk and the nonsense. I am a man of action"
—BENITO MUSSOLINI

**SWASTIKA**

## Nazism

Nazis were Fascists who also believed in the superiority of Aryans (white, non-Jewish people, ideally blond with blue eyes). They thought they had the right to enslave "inferior" peoples. Their symbol was the swastika.

**Key points**

| | |
|---|---|
| *Origins:* | Hitler put forward the founding ideas of Nazism in his book *Mein Kampf* (1925) |
| *Children were taught:* | The Aryan race is supreme |
| *Led by:* | A dictator |
| *Most influential group:* | The military, to expand the German state and form a new empire called the Third Reich |
| *Opposed to:* | Jews, non-whites, and Communism |

Nazi Germany

### Germany and Adolf Hitler
Even though he was Austrian, Hitler believed that the Aryan master race should build a new German empire.

**ADOLF HITLER**

| | |
|---|---|
| *Lived:* | 20 April 1889– 30 April 1945 |
| *Led:* | Germany (1933–45) |
| *Nickname:* | The Führer ("the Leader") |

## "What we have to fight for is . . . the freedom and independence of the Fatherland"
—ADOLF HITLER

### Two dictators
Hitler (centre) and Mussolini (left) were allies but did not fully trust each other.

# Communism

**HAMMER AND SICKLE**

According to Communism, all property and businesses should be owned by the people. Its hammer and sickle symbol represents industry and farming, showing that factory workers and farmers can work together.

## Key points

| | |
|---|---|
| *Origins:* | Karl Marx developed the idea of Communism in his manifesto in 1848 |
| *Children were taught:* | No one has his or her own private property |
| *Led by:* | The Communist Party (often led by a dictator) |
| *Most influential group:* | Party leaders |
| *Opposed to:* | Capitalism (a free economy) |

### Communist Soviet Union

### Soviet Union and Joseph Stalin
The Soviet Union (or USSR) formed in 1922. From 1924, Joseph Stalin began to take over.

**JOSEPH STALIN**

| | |
|---|---|
| *Lived:* | 18 December 1878– 5 March 1953 |
| *Led:* | Soviet Union (1924–53) |
| *Nickname:* | Vozhd ("the Boss") |

## "From each according to his ability, to each according to his **needs**"
—JOSEPH STALIN

# Democracy

**BALLOT BOX**

In democracies, people vote every few years for political representatives. Those with the most votes make, pass, or veto laws. Everyone has the right to express his or her own opinions.

## Key points

| | |
|---|---|
| *Origins:* | The ancient Greeks were the first known to elect leaders |
| *Children were taught:* | Freedom and equality are vital |
| *Led by:* | A president or prime minister from an elected party |
| *Most influential groups:* | Lawmakers and voters |
| *Opposed to:* | Dictatorships |

### Democracy and the world
By the 1930s, there were many democratic countries, such as the United States, led by President Roosevelt, and the United Kingdom.

**FRANKLIN D. ROOSEVELT**

| | |
|---|---|
| *Lived:* | 30 January 1882– 12 April 1945 |
| *Led:* | United States (1933–45) |
| *Nickname:* | FDR |

## "As I would not be a slave, so I would not be a master. This expresses my idea of **democracy**"
—ABRAHAM LINCOLN

# Militarism

Japan was led by Emperor Hirohito from 1929, but its real rulers were the heads of the army. Under this strong military rule, Japan wanted to expand into China and Southeast Asia, conquering European colonies to build its own empire. Japan's slogan was "Asia for the Asians".

### Rising sun
This military flag shows the rays from Japan's rising sun symbol, spreading out to reach new territory.

### Fighting for new lands
Eager to expand, Japan had fought and won against the Russians in Manchuria and Korea, from 1904 to 1905, and went to war with China in 1937.

# Blitzkrieg [Lightning war]

Germany conquered Poland in September 1939 with blitzkrieg ("lightning war") tactics. After an eight-month delay in military action – the "Phoney War" – the Germans suddenly swept across Europe.

## Military buildup

Germany's quick victories were the result of years of preparation. From 1933 to 1939, Hitler increased the German army tenfold, to 1 million soldiers. His air force grew from 36 to 8,250 planes, and his navy from 30 to 95 warships.

Germany

### Plans for expansion

Adolf Hitler planned to take over countries bordering Germany and use their "inferior" citizens as slave labour. He expected Britain to negotiate for peace.

| May 1940 | Germany | Allies |
|---|---|---|
| Divisions | 154 | 144 |
| Armored vehicles | 4,000 | 4,000 |
| Fighter planes | 1,100 | 1,100 |
| Bombers | 1,100 | 400 |
| Dive-bombers | 400 | 0 |

### Opposing forces

The German army had more up-to-date equipment than the Allied forces of Britain, France, and Belgium. The Allies' resources were also spread very thin.

INVADED:
**10 MAY 1940**
SURRENDERED:
**28 MAY 1940**

**9**

**55**

**630**

### Belgium

After overpowering the 630 soldiers defending the strategic fortress of Eben-Emael, German forces rolled across Belgium. The capital, Brussels, fell in May.

**BRUSSELS**

BELGIUM

Eben-Emael

### Capturing Eben-Emael

*Gliders landed 55 paratroopers armed with flamethrowers to take this key Belgian fortress.*

## Panzer (tank) division

**123 TANKS**

A German tank division was made up of panzers and their crews, support staff, and equipment. The exact numbers varied, but a typical tank division in 1940 included:

**1,402 TRUCKS**

**561 PASSENGER VEHICLES**

**421 ARMOURED VEHICLES**

**1,280 MOTORCYCLES**

**394 OFFICERS**

**1,962 NON-COMMISSIONED OFFICERS**

**9,321 SOLDIERS**

Ardennes Forest

PARIS

FRANCE

INVADED:
**12 MAY 1940**
SURRENDERED:
**22 JUNE 1940**

### France

German tanks passed through the hilly, dense Ardennes Forest – to the surprise of the French. Pushing over roads clogged with terrified refugees, the invaders reached Paris on 14 June.

### French prisoners

1,575,600 prisoners were taken to Germany to work as slave labour.

**Infantry**
*Foot soldiers carried machine guns or other hand weapons.*

**Motorized infantry**
*Trucks and other vehicles moved quickly into areas cleared by the tanks.*

**Bombers**
*Large bombers destroyed bridges, roads, and railways.*

**Tanks**
*These stayed in groups, so they had enormous firepower.*

**Dive-bombers**
*With their wailing sirens, these terrified troops and refugees.*

## Lightning attacks

Blitzkrieg was a burst of fast, powerful attacks, designed to knock out the enemy. Dive-bombers screamed down on airfields, while tanks punched holes in enemy lines. Then the infantry surrounded the remaining, isolated defenders.

Calendar days between invasion and surrender

**1 SEPTEMBER 1939**

**INVADED:**
1 SEPT. 1939
**SURRENDERED:**
27 SEPT. 1939

WARSAW

## POLAND

**INVADED:**
10 MAY 1940
**SURRENDERED:**
15 MAY 1940

**INVADED:**
10 MAY 1940
**SURRENDERED:**
11 MAY 1940

**Netherlands**
German paratroopers were dropped in to smooth the way for the ground forces. After the Luftwaffe (air force) bombing of Rotterdam left 80,000 people homeless, the Dutch surrendered, fearing more attacks.

AMSTERDAM
ROTTERDAM
NETHERLANDS

LUXEMBOURG

**Luxembourg**
With no army, neutral Luxembourg didn't stand a chance. It took just three hours for three German panzer divisions to rumble the 48 km (30 miles) across this tiny country.

**Poland**
Poland could not defend its long border against the Reich. Hitler had a pact to share Poland with the Soviet Union; Stalin invaded on 17 September. Warsaw surrendered on 27 September.

# 1,308

**Deadly drop**
*The Germans dropped 1,308 bombs on the Dutch port of Rotterdam.*

GERMAN 8,082

GERMAN

POLISH

Polish 95,000

**DEAD: 103,082**

## 47,000

German 27,278

Polish 130,000

**WOUNDED: 157,278**

**940,000 remained until 1945**

24,600 prisoners died

71,000 escaped

320,000

220,000

Released to Vichy regime (see right)

Released for disability or sickness

**Paris, France**
Hitler kept the capital under German control but allowed southern France to govern itself until 11 November 1942, when Vichy France was occupied.

**Refugees**
*47,000 people fled from Luxembourg to France. They didn't realize that the Germans were heading there, too.*

**Heavy Polish losses**
In the invasion, 12 Poles died for every 1 German. Nearly 5 times as many Polish people were wounded.

## "The small countries are simply smashed up, one by one, like matchwood"

—WINSTON CHURCHILL'S MESSAGE TO FRANKLIN D. ROOSEVELT, 15 MAY 1940

## Refugees

The fighting and the threat of Nazi rule terrified millions of people who were in the path of the invasion. Many, like this French family, packed as many possessions as they could and fled on the dusty roads. Leaving behind homes, jobs, and normal life, refugees faced hardships and danger. Many were even attacked by German dive-bombers.

# The**a**tres of w**a**r [Worldwide]

**Europe and the Atlantic**
Hitler conquered much of western Europe in 1940 and tried to starve Britain by stopping supplies from coming across the Atlantic. In 1941, he headed east to begin a drawn-out battle for the Soviet Union. (See chapter two.)

PACIFIC OCEAN

CANADA

NORTH AMERICA

UNITED STATES

EUR

TUNISIA

MOROCCO

ALGERIA

AFR

NORTH ATLANTIC OCEAN

SOUTH AMERICA

SOUTH ATLANTIC OCEAN

World War II was not one single war – it was many separate wars all around the world, between the Axis powers (Germany, Italy, and Japan) and the Allies (including Britain and the USA). More than 100 countries were involved in the fighting, which took place in different theatres, or areas, of war. This map shows the main theatres of conflict in November 1942.

•1939  •1940  •1941

EUROPE & THE ATLANTIC
AFRICA & THE MIDDLE EAST
THE PACIFIC

**Key events of the war**
The Axis powers advanced from 1939 to 1942 but were slowly defeated, at a cost of millions of lives.

**1940** *The British air victory in the Battle of Britain put a stop to Hitler's western advance.*

**1941** *Japan's attempt to destroy the US Pacific Fleet in the naval base at Pearl Harbor, HI, brought the United States into the war.*

## MAP KEY
1. Ireland  2. Britain
3. Portugal  4. Spain
5. France  6. Belgium
7. Netherlands  8. Luxembourg
9. Switzerland  10. Italy
11. Sardinia  12. Germany
13. Denmark  14. Norway
15. Sweden  16. Finland
17. Estonia  18. Latvia
19. Lithuania  20. East Prussia
21. Poland  22. Czechoslovakia
23. Austria  24. Hungary
25. Romania  26. Yugoslavia
27. Albania  28. Greece
29. Bulgaria  30. Turkey

### The Pacific
Japan attacked China
in 1937, then more Asian
and Pacific lands in 1941,
forcing the USA into the war.
Early successes in 1942 were
countered by a long, hard fight
until 1945. (See chapter three.)

### Africa and the Middle East
Italy attacked in Africa in
1940 and was joined by German
forces in 1941. One target was
the valuable oil fields of the
Middle East, then controlled by
Britain. Axis forces were pushed
back in 1943. (See chapter four.)

## MAP KEY
Allied powers
Under Axis control
Neutral countries

•1942     •1943     •1944     •1945

**1942** *The US naval victory at the Battle of Midway stopped Japanese advances. Then the Allies began the long push toward Tokyo.*

**1943** *On the eastern front, Germany was forced into retreat after losing at Stalingrad in the Soviet Union.*

**1945** *Allied advances from both east and west forced a German surrender on 7 May. Atomic bombs helped end the war with Japan on 14 August.*

# Europ
# Atlant

- Which air attacks reduced British cities to rubble?

* Why did some Jewish families go into hiding?

- Which were the deadliest WWII submarines?

& the

ic war

# War in Europe [German

In 1940, Adolf Hitler's forces carved a swathe across western Europe in a matter of weeks. When they reached the coast, they began to attack Britain from the air. Then Hitler suddenly headed east, towards his former ally, the Soviet Union.

## 27 MAY–4 JUNE 1940
### Dunkirk evacuation
At the end of May, 338,000 British, French, and Belgian soldiers were trapped on the coast of France. They were rescued by a flotilla of ships and boats from England.

BRITISH SOLDIERS WAITING TO BE TAKEN OFF THE BEACH AT DUNKIRK

## JAN. 1940
### Rationing
Food rationing was introduced in Britain, and other fighting nations followed suit. Later, fuel and clothes were also rationed for the war effort.

BRITISH RATION BOOKS FROM 1940–41 AND 1947–48

**JUNE 1940**
*German U-boats began sinking huge numbers of ships carrying supplies to Britain across the Atlantic.*

**10 JUNE 1940**
*Thinking that Hitler would win, Mussolini declared war on Britain and France.*

**14 JUNE 1940**
*German troops marched into Paris. Millions of refugees headed for southern France.*

## • 1940 •

*Dots represent monthly increases until 1941.*

**APR. 1940**
*Germany invaded Denmark and Norway.*

**10 MAY 1940**
*German tanks rolled into Belgium and the Netherlands.*

**12 MAY 1940**
*German troops advanced into France.*

**14 MAY 1940**
*Britain created a volunteer defence force, later called the Home Guard.*

**7 SEPT. 1940**
*Hitler began the Blitz – eight months of bombing Britain's cities, ports, and factories.*

## JULY–OCT. 1940
### Battle of Britain
Germany tried but failed to destroy Britain's air force ahead of an invasion. This was the start of a 16-week struggle for superiority called the Battle of Britain.

GERMAN STUKAS RETURNING FROM A DIVE-BOMBING RAID

## 10 MAY 1940
### Churchill
Winston Churchill became Britain's new prime minister after Neville Chamberlain resigned. Churchill's speeches helped inspire British people to fight the Nazis, and his military expertise and tactical know-how were invaluable.

**WINSTON CHURCHILL**
Prime minister, Britain

| | |
|---|---|
| In power: | 1940–45 |
| Led: | Coalition government |

# 1,400 barrage balloons
## protected British cities during the Blitz

## DEC. 1940
### T-34 tank enters service
Soviet tank factories began building the T-34, one of the most effective tanks of the war. Enemy shells simply bounced off the sloping armour of these fast, powerful metal giants.

A SOVIET
T-34 TANK

## DEC. 1941
### The Holocaust
The Nazis opened the first death camp. Millions of Jews, whom the Nazis considered "inferior", were killed in these camps.

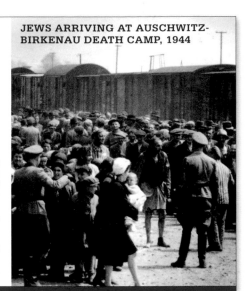

JEWS ARRIVING AT AUSCHWITZ-BIRKENAU DEATH CAMP, 1944

**6 million: the number of European Jews killed in the Holocaust**

## SEPT. 1941
*The German army sealed off the Soviet city of Leningrad and starved its people for 872 days.*

## OCT. 1941
*The Battle of Moscow began as German forces threatened the Soviet capital.*

## 17 MAY 1943
*British planes dropped bouncing bombs on German dams in the Dambuster Raid.*

## •1941    •1942    •1943    1944•

*Dots represent yearly increases.*

## 11 MAR. 1941
*The Lend-Lease Act allowed the USA to supply Allied forces.*

## AUG. 1941
*A young woman named Andrée de Jongh set up the Comet Line, a rescue route for shot-down Allied airmen.*

## 30 MAY 1942
*More than 1,000 British planes bombed and destroyed the German city of Cologne.*

## AUG. 1942
*The battle for the Soviet city of Stalingrad began. It lasted through the freezing winter.*

## 19 APR. 1943
*Jews rebelled against the Nazis in the Warsaw Ghetto uprising.*

## MAY 1941
### Enigma
Aided by Poles, British code crackers were able to decrypt messages sent by Enigma, a German encoding machine. Finally, the Allies could read messages sent to and from U-boats.

THE GERMAN
ENIGMA MACHINE

## JUNE–DEC. 1941
### Operation Barbarossa
Soviet leader Joseph Stalin was horrified when Germany broke its peace pact. About 4 million German troops advanced into the Soviet Union as Hitler switched his attack to the east.

GERMANS ADVANCING PAST
A BLAZING SOVIET TRUCK

If Hitler wanted to invade Britain, he would first have to gain control of the skies over southern England. So the Luftwaffe sent its speedy Me 109 fighter planes to face British Spitfires and Hurricanes. The Battle of Britain was fought from 10 July to 31 October 1940.

| Hurricane specifications | |
|---|---|
| *Top speed* | 523 kph (325 mph) |
| *Range* | 965 km (600 miles) |
| *Maximum altitude* | 10,365 m (34,000 ft) |
| *Wingspan* | 12 m (40 ft) |
| *Armament* | 8 machine guns |
| *Number built* | 14,533 |

**Hood**
*This was built from the newly invented bulletproof material Perspex.*

**Tail fin**
*The rounded tail fin and large rudder allowed the plane to make tight turns.*

**Tail wheel**
*This wheel did not tuck in during flight.*

**Machine guns**
*The pilot fired the four guns by pushing a button in short bursts.*

## Dogfights

When German planes crossed the English Channel to attack British radar stations and airfields, Royal Air Force (RAF) pilots took off to intercept them. Groups of planes had deadly dogfights, performing desperate corkscrew turns and dives. Each tried to get behind an enemy plane and fire a blast of bullets or shells to rip it apart and send it spiralling downwards.

**Wing**
*The aluminium covering was lightweight but strong.*

**Propeller**
*Three metal blades sliced through the air.*

**Hawker Hurricane**
Hurricanes claimed more than half of the German planes shot down in the Battle of Britain. They could be rearmed, refuelled, and ready to return to the skies in just nine minutes.

## Scramble!

Between fights, pilots tried to rest. Then the next warning would come in, and they would "scramble", running to their planes. Sometimes they flew five missions in a single day. Their biggest fear was being burned alive in a shot-down plane.

**Ready to fly**
A British pilot wore leather headgear that had a built-in oxygen mask and radio.

Returning radio wave

AIRCRAFT

Outgoing radio wave

SENDER/ RECEIVER

**How radar helped**
Radar sends out radio waves that bounce back off objects such as planes. This vital tool allowed the British to detect enemy planes before they came into sight.

**Me 109 specifications**

| | |
|---|---|
| Top speed | 640 kph (398 mph) |
| Range | 850 km (530 miles) |
| Maximum altitude | 11,880 m (39,370 ft) |
| Wingspan | 10 m (32.5 ft) |
| Armament | 2 machine guns, 1 cannon |
| Number built | 32,984 |

## "Never in the field of human conflict was **so much** owed by so many to so few"—WINSTON CHURCHILL

**Pilot**
*The pilot's heated flying suit plugged into the cockpit.*

**Front cannon**
*Shells were fired through the propeller.*

**Frame**
*The plane was made of thin, light metal to reduce drag.*

**Fuel tank**
*This held enough fuel for a flight just over an hour long.*

**Wing**
*The wings were thin and light, with special slats that provided more control during dives.*

**Engine**
*The fuel-injected engine was better at handling dives than that of a British plane.*

**Messerschmitt Bf 109**
Known as the Me 109 for short, this sleek fighter could climb and dive faster than its British rivals, but it did not turn as well. The Luftwaffe relied on about 33,000 Me 109s.

**Wing gun**
*Bullets for this gun were fed from the fuselage, to keep the wings light.*

## Dunkirk

In late May 1940, the Germans had the British, French, and Belgian forces pinned down and at their mercy on the French coast, near Dunkirk. A rescue fleet was sent across the English Channel before Hitler had a chance to attack. The 861 boats ferried 338,000 troops back to Britain. They had to abandon their equipment – but they were safe!

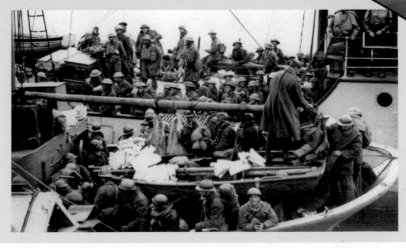

**Little ships**
Troops waded through choppy waters in their heavy uniforms to reach their rescuers. Small fishing and sailing boats shuttled the men to destroyers and other large craft.

# The Blitz

For eight months from 7 September, 1940, the Germans rained down bombs on Britain's cities. The Blitz left 43,000 people dead and 250,000 homeless. A night for a typical family might have gone like this:

**6:00 PM** — Blackout curtains are closed so that lights inside the house won't help bombers find a target.

**6:30 PM** — The family puts an emergency bag by the door. It contains a torch, candles, matches, blankets, ration books, gas masks, and ID cards.

**8:00 PM** — The air-raid siren wails. Radar has detected bombers over the English Channel.

**8:10 PM** — The family leaves the doors of the house open, to limit the effects of a blast. In the garden, they hurry down the steps of an air-raid shelter.

**8:20 PM** — Anti-aircraft guns clatter at the bombers, aided by searchlights. The family hears the whistle of falling high-explosive bombs and the wail of fire engines.

**10:30 PM** — The next wave of planes releases high explosives, and the shelter rattles with each blast.

**5:00 AM** — The two-minute "all clear" siren sounds. The family finds their house unscathed – this time.

**7:00 AM** — The clean-up begins: sweeping glass, digging out bodies, and tending to the injured, while children rush to add to their shrapnel collections.

## 177,000 people slept on underground train platforms

# R sistanc [The underground]

Across Europe, individuals risked their lives with small acts of resistance – such as cutting phone lines – against the occupying Germans. Soon these individuals banded together to become more organized groups.

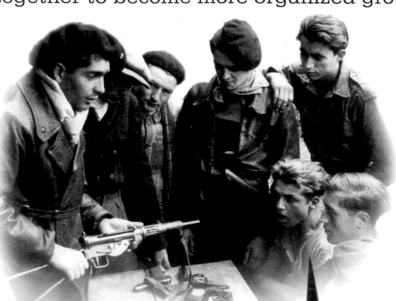

## Fighting back

Resistance groups fought back in many ways, from printing anti-Nazi leaflets to kidnapping or killing German officers. They also smuggled out information about targets the Allies should bomb.

**Truck stoppers**
Spiked caltrops were placed on roads to puncture the tyres of vehicles in enemy convoys.

**Control switches**
*These set the volume and tone so that messages could be heard clearly.*

## SOE messages

Unoccupied Britain set up the Special Operations Executive (SOE) to support resistance movements across Europe and, later, in Japanese-occupied Asia. Its male and female operatives often parachuted in to help, organize, and equip these "secret armies", keeping in touch using covert radios.

**Headphones**
*These allowed radio operators to work without being overheard.*

**CLAM MINE**

**DETONATOR**

**Magnet**
*This attached the mine to a metal surface.*

## Sabotage

Members of the resistance made life harder for the German army by blocking roads, blowing up bridges and tunnels, and wrecking railways. Damaging the transport system slowed down the movement of enemy troops and weapons.

**Clam mine**
This mine consisted of high explosives and a powerful magnet, which was designed to stick to a bridge or railway line. It could be detonated remotely.

**Copper coil**
*This tuning coil was used to find the wavelength of incoming messages.*

## Helping heroes

The resistance network gave food and shelter to airmen who had been shot down. Pilots usually trekked south to British-run Gibaltrar for journeys home.

### Radio codes

*Anyone could tune in to radio transmissions, so messages had to be sent in code.*

### Suitcase disguise

This secret radio was made by the SOE for use in France. The case hid it from prying eyes, but it didn't make it easy to carry – it weighed 13.5 kg (30 lbs)!

### Resistance heroine

From Vichy, in central France, Fourcade led the Alliance, a network of 3,000 agents.

**MARIE-MADELEINE FOURCADE**

| Code name: Hedgehog | |
|---|---|
| Lived: | 1909–89 |
| Resistance leader: | 1941–45 |

### Silk maps

Allied airmen were issued with silk maps to help guide them if they were shot down. Unlike paper, silk didn't rip or fall apart if it got wet.

## "Who will ever suspect a woman?"

—GEORGES LOUSTAUNAU-LACAU, THE MAN WHO RECRUITED MARIE-MADELEINE FOURCADE

### Spare valves

*Valves were tubes of thin glass that controlled the electricity supply.*

DUTCH RESISTANCE

NORWEGIAN RESISTANCE

FRENCH RESISTANCE

### Batteries

*These provided back-up power in remote places with no electricity.*

### Morse tap

*Tapping this produced two different clicks for sending messages in Morse code.*

## To resist or not?

There were resistance movements in every occupied country, but not everyone resisted. Most people simply waited out the war, while others collaborated with the Nazis.

### Armband ID

When the Allies invaded, resistance fighters identified themselves with armbands like these.

# The eastern front [Attack

On 22 June 1941, Hitler switched his attack from western to eastern Europe. He broke his peace pact with Stalin and invaded the Soviet Union with a force of 4 million troops. Hitler wanted to control the country's resources, rule its "inferior" peoples, defeat Communism, and kill Russian Jews. However, just six months later, outside Moscow, the Germans were forced to retreat.

## "It is the Führer's unshakeable decision to raze Moscow and Leningrad to the ground"
—GERMAN SUPREME COMMAND, 1941

### The invasion
The Germans advanced quickly, thanks to their state-of-the-art weapons. In just three months, they had killed or captured 3 million of the poorly equipped Soviet troops.

## Operation Barbarossa
Hitler's plan was to capture and occupy the Soviet Union in the summer, when travel was easy on dry roads. Targets were major cities, oil fields, coal fields, and farms that could supply the Third Reich with fuel and food.

LENINGRAD
8 Sept. 1941

MOSCOW
13 Oct. 1941

GERMAN ATTACKS

R U S S I A

STALINGRAD
23 Aug. 1942

### Divided attack
Germany pushed forwards towards the key cities of Leningrad, Moscow, and Stalingrad. Its forces were spread too thinly to conquer them.

# on the Red Army]

## Turning the tide

The Soviet Union's Red Army fought out of pride for their country – and fear. Stalin had ordered that those who deserted or surrendered would be shot, and their families punished. Slowly, the Soviets pushed the Germans back.

### Supplying the army

Stalin moved munitions factories east, away from the fighting. The labourers worked gruelling 18-hour shifts to keep the army supplied.

## Rifle power

Hidden Soviet snipers could fire on enemy soldiers up to 365 m (1,200 ft) away. They worked in pairs. One acted as a lookout, and the other fired shots. Then they swapped.

### Girl power

About 2,000 Red Army snipers were young women.

### Weapon of choice

The Mosin-Nagant 1891/30 was the most often used Soviet sniper rifle.

### Telescopic sight

*This sight made the target appear about four times nearer.*

### Front sight

*This sight helped the sniper line up his or her target more accurately.*

### Trigger

*Pulling and releasing this fired the rifle.*

### Magazine

*The ammunition cartridge went here.*

# Stalingrad

The Battle of Stalingrad, which began in the summer of 1942, was fought in a ruined city through the freezing winter. The Soviet victory, at the terrible cost of 490,000 Soviet and German lives, marked the first time Hitler's forces had to retreat.

**23 AUG.** — Luftwaffe bombs turned much of the city to rubble and killed around 47,000 people. Some women and children were evacuated, but Stalin wanted Stalingrad's civilians to stay and fight.

**13 SEPT.** — German troops reached the city centre. Snipers were as useful as tanks in combat, because the battle was fought street by street and house by house.

**19 NOV.** — 1 million Red Army troops began to encircle and bombard the Germans.

**23 NOV.** — 275,000 German soldiers and 50,000 Soviet civilians were trapped for the winter. Vital supplies of food, fuel, and ammunition had to be dropped into the city by plane. Many people died from starvation, frostbite, or disease.

**JAN. 1943** — The Soviets captured two key German airfields, preventing the delivery of crucial supplies.

**31 JAN.** — The 91,000 Germans still alive surrendered and were taken prisoner. Only 10,000 Soviet civilians survived. These included 904 children, only 9 of whom ever found their parents again.

**2 FEB.** — The German prisoners were marched east to Siberia. Tens of thousands died on the journey.

**99%**
of Stalingrad's buildings were destroyed in the siege

# The Holocaust

When the Nazis came to power, more than 9 million Jewish people were living across Europe. In eastern Europe, they spoke Yiddish, and Yiddish culture thrived. Throughout Europe, they were successful in every walk of life. But anti-Semitism was common, and Hitler and the Nazis were able to implement a plan of genocide, or mass murder.

**90%** of Polish Jews were killed in the Holocaust

## Nazi camps

Starting in 1933, violence toward Jews intensified. The Nazis established concentration camps and forced-labour camps to detain Jews and others considered a danger to the regime. Across Europe, Jews were herded into areas called ghettos, to control them and prepare them for the camps.

Hidden
Some Jewish families – including, famously, the family of Anne Frank – tried to hide. This hiding-place is in Haarlem, the Netherlands.

## The Final Solution

The Final Solution, the plan to exterminate the Jewish people, entered its deadliest phase in 1941. In Russia, more than 1 million Jews were rounded up and shot. In 1942, extermination camps were used to kill millions of Jews and other "inferior" people, such as Communists, Roma (gypsies), and homosexuals. Jews were herded like cattle onto trains and transported to the camps to be gassed to death.

Yellow star
*This patch identified its wearer as Jewish.*

A culture disappears
The Jewish populations of Europe fell shockingly because of Nazi repression and killings.

| Jewish populations in Europe | | |
|---|---|---|
| | Pre–Final Solution population | Killed in Final Solution |
| Poland | 3,300,000 | 3,000,000 |
| Soviet Union | 2,850,000 | 1,252,000 |
| Hungary | 650,000 | 450,000 |
| Romania | 600,000 | 300,000 |
| Baltic countries | 253,000 | 228,000 |
| Germany and Austria | 240,000 | 210,000 |

# Solution]

## Rising up

By spring 1943, with many of their relatives and friends already sent to the death camps, Jewish people in the Warsaw ghetto launched an uprising against the Nazis. But it was a hopeless fight.

## Eyewitness

**NAME:** Jürgen Stroop

**DATE:** 1943

**LOCATION:** Warsaw, Poland

**DETAILS:** Stroop was a loyal Nazi who joined Hitler's personal guard unit, the Waffen-SS. He held the rank of major general at the time he was sent to Poland, on 17 April 1943, to deal with the Warsaw ghetto uprising.

❝ On 23 April . . . [we were ordered] to complete the combing out of the Warsaw ghetto with the greatest severity and relentless tenacity. I therefore decided to destroy the entire Jewish residential area by setting every block on fire. ❞

## More here

*For key to symbols, see page 112*

***Survivors: True Stories of Children in the Holocaust***
by Allan Zullo and Mara Bovsun

***I Have Lived a Thousand Years: Growing Up in the Holocaust***
by Livia Bitton-Jackson

***The Diary of a Young Girl***
by Anne Frank

In the Netherlands, visit homes where Jews hid: the **Anne Frank House** and the **Corrie ten Boom Museum**.

**Auschwitz-Birkenau Memorial** is on the site of the concentration camp in Poland.

See the collections at the **United States Holocaust Memorial Museum**, Washington, D.C., and the **Jewish Museum**, New York.

**anti-Semitism:** prejudice against or hatred of Jews.

**concentration camp:** a large compound where civilians, especially Jews, were kept in very harsh conditions. In some camps, also known as extermination or death camps, the prisoners were deliberately killed.

**genocide:** the systematic murder of many people from the same racial or cultural group.

**ghetto:** a section of a city, often a highly populated slum area, where Jews were made to live by the Nazis during World War II.

### Pre-war life

This picture shows Jewish children in the city of Lodz, Poland, in 1930. Their parents may have worked in the textile or construction industries. They lived ordinary lives: attending public schools, playing sports, and going to Yiddish theatres. The Lodz Jewish community, numbering more than 230,000, was completely wiped out during the Holocaust.

The Nazis and their allies murdered 1.5 million children in death camps in less than four years. Most children arrived with relatives, often with their whole families. Nearly all those who were under ten years old were killed on arrival. The rest were put to work, often dying from disease or starvation or in random killings. Some of the children's names and the ages at which they died are printed here.

## Eyewitness

**"Most people who entered through the gates of Auschwitz-Birkenau were confronted with an immediate 'selection'; either to be admitted to the camp or to be killed by gas on arrival."**

**NAME:** Kitty Hart-Moxon
**LOCATION:** Poland
**DETAILS:** Born into a Jewish family, Kitty Hart-Moxon survived a ghetto, the massacre of Jews at Belzec in Poland, and prison. In 1943, she was sent to the Auschwitz concentration camp. In 1945, as the Germans retreated, she and hundreds of other women were forcibly marched through Germany and Czechoslovakia. Most died on the journey. She was freed by American soldiers and went to live in England.

**❝** Most people who entered through the gates of Auschwitz-Birkenau were confronted with an immediate 'selection'; either to be admitted to the camp or to be killed by gas on arrival. We were marched to be stripped, shaved of all hair, and tattooed on our left forearms. From then on we had no names. I was now number 39934 and my mother, 39933.

There was no water to wash [with] or drink, and no lavatories. The small bread ration was handed out after evening roll call and the camp soup, at midday. It would not sustain life for very long.

For many months I worked in dozens of work groups: loading dead bodies, digging trenches, or working in potato fields, which enabled me to smuggle some potatoes back into the camp.

There was an epidemic of typhus. Most people did not survive when they fell ill, as treatment was non-existent. But I was taken to my mother, who looked after me and hid me during the daily selections for the gas chambers.

We witnessed the killing of more than half a million people. We girls could not take in what was happening – even though we heard the screams as people were dying. But it sank in eventually when we saw the people disappear before our eyes, never to be seen again, except for the piles of belongings left behind. **❞**

"I believe in the Sun,
even when it is not shining.
And I believe in love,
even when there's no one there.
And I believe in God,
even when he is silent.

May there someday be sunshine.
May there someday be happiness.
May there someday be love.
May there someday be peace."

—CARVED ON A WALL BY AN UNKNOWN
VICTIM OF THE HOLOCAUST

Britain imported huge amounts of food and other vital materials from the United States, Canada, and many other countries. Hitler tried to force an early end to the war by blocking the convoys of cargo ships ferrying these goods across the Atlantic. His weapon was a fleet of U-boats (submarines).

## Save everything!

Factories across Britain switched to making planes, tanks, and munitions for the war effort. But materials were in short supply. The government organized salvage drives to collect scrap metal, paper, glass bottles, and rags.

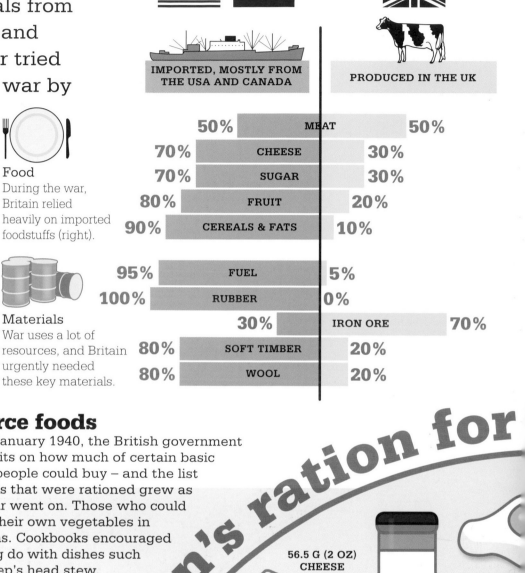

**IMPORTED, MOSTLY FROM THE USA AND CANADA**

**PRODUCED IN THE UK**

**Food**
During the war, Britain relied heavily on imported foodstuffs (right).

| IMPORTED | | PRODUCED |
|---|---|---|
| 50% | MEAT | 50% |
| 70% | CHEESE | 30% |
| 70% | SUGAR | 30% |
| 80% | FRUIT | 20% |
| 90% | CEREALS & FATS | 10% |

**Materials**
War uses a lot of resources, and Britain urgently needed these key materials.

| IMPORTED | | PRODUCED |
|---|---|---|
| 95% | FUEL | 5% |
| 100% | RUBBER | 0% |
| 30% | IRON ORE | 70% |
| 80% | SOFT TIMBER | 20% |
| 80% | WOOL | 20% |

## Scarce foods

From January 1940, the British government set limits on how much of certain basic foods people could buy – and the list of foods that were rationed grew as the war went on. Those who could grew their own vegetables in gardens. Cookbooks encouraged making do with dishes such as sheep's head stew.

**The Land Army**
With male farmworkers away at the front, women were drafted to help. By 1944, more than 80,000 "land girls" were planting and harvesting crops.

Foods people grew during the war:
Cauliflower • Potatoes
Carrots • Turnips
Parsnips • Beetroot
Runner beans
Leeks

Foods in extremely short supply:
Bananas • Oranges
Lemons • Fresh peaches
Grapes • Pineapples
Onions

**1 person's ration for**

56.5 G (2 OZ) CHEESE

568 ML (1 PT) MILK

56.5 G (2 OZ) SWEETS

113 G (4 OZ) JAM

# war]

## Defensive formation

Allied cargo ships travelled in convoys, with escorts of naval ships to fight off submarine attacks. It was desperately important but dangerous work to zigzag across sometimes stormy seas.

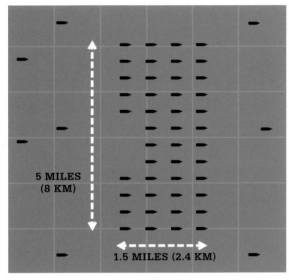

5 MILES (8 KM)

1.5 MILES (2.4 KM)

**An Atlantic convoy**
About 45 ships would travel in formation, with 8 protective escorts around them.

1939
1940
1941
1942
1943
1944
1945

0   500   1,000   1,500   2,000   2,500

### Torpedo attacks
German U-boats torpedoed the convoys. If one ship was hit, the others slowed down to rescue the survivors.

## Building for safety

The number of ships sunk by U-boats reached its peak in 1942, with more than 1,500 lost. But starting in 1943, the tables turned. Intensive US shipbuilding paid off, and larger convoys more successfully countered the German threat.

**KEY**
US ships built
Allied ships sunk

# 1 week in July 1942

1 EGG

113 G (4 OZ) BUTTER

56.5 G (2 OZ) TEA

226 G (8 OZ) SUGAR

113 G (4 OZ) BACON

56.5 G (2 OZ) CHOCOLATE

## Nazi rations

Food energy is measured in calories – an adult needs 1,200 calories a day to avoid starvation. In Germany, food was fairly plentiful, but still rationed. In neighbouring occupied Poland, supplies were lower, and the Nazis set limits for different groups.

**2,310** GERMANS

**1,790** FOREIGNERS

**654** POLES

**184** JEWS

### Calorie quotas
Poles were on starvation rations, and Jews faced painful deaths, since they received only 7.5 percent of the nutrition they needed.

# U-boat [Underwater killer]

U-boats were German submarines that attacked Allied merchant vessels crossing the Atlantic. Feared by the Allies, they were also a dangerous place for their crews. More than two-thirds of all U-boat sailors died at sea.

**U-boat pens**
Many U-boats were based in harbours from France to Norway. Their missions could last weeks or even months.

## Dead shot

U-boats (from the German for "undersea boat") spent most of their time on the surface, where they could move faster and visibility was better. When they found a target, they usually attacked at night, under the cover of darkness. They fired underwater missiles called torpedoes.

**Line of torpedo fire**

**U-boat**

**Supply convoy**
*Allied ships travelled in convoys (groups) for protection.*

**Wolf-pack tactics**
U-boats hunted in packs, picking off one target at a time.

**Conning tower**
*Two lookouts worked from the tower when the U-boat was on the surface.*

**Deck gun**
*The large deck gun could fire 15 cannon rounds a minute and was used to finish off enemy boats.*

**Net cutter**
*This cut through enemy anti-submarine nets.*

**Radio room**
*Coded messages were sent and received here.*

**Torpedo tubes**
*Deadly torpedoes were launched from these.*

**Stern chamber**
*Flooding this chamber added weight and kept the boat stable.*

**Toilet**
*Waste was hand pumped into the sea.*

**Bunk beds**
*The crew slept in shifts, taking turns using the beds.*

**Spare torpedoes**
*After these were launched, this space was used for folding beds.*

**Two periscopes**
*The front periscope scanned the horizon for ships and planes. The rear one aimed torpedoes.*

**Rear torpedo tube**
*This launched missiles from the back of the U-boat.*

**Twin rudders**
*These allowed the boat to turn tightly.*

**Propellers**
*The propellers drove the U-boat forwards or backwards.*

**Hatch**
*This was closed during dives.*

**Electric motors**
*The boat relied on these when underwater.*

**Diesel engines**
*On the surface, the boat was powered by two engines.*

**Galley**
*Food was prepared on hot plates and in two small ovens.*

**Batteries**
*The electric motors ran on rechargeable batteries.*

**Ballast tanks**
*Distributed around the boat, these tanks were filled or emptied to make the submarine fall or rise.*

**Control room**
*The captain and key equipment were based here.*

**Destroyer escort**
*Warships like this one were designed to track, chase, and attack submarines.*

| Type VIIC specifications | |
|---|---|
| *Introduced* | 1940 |
| *Number made* | 709 |
| *Crew members* | 44 |
| *Length* | 67 m (220 ft) |
| *Speed on the surface* | 17 knots (31 kph / 20 mph) |
| *Surface range* | 13,680 km (8,500 miles) |
| *Speed underwater* | 7.6 knots (14 kph / 8.7 mph) |
| *Underwater range* | 130 km (80 miles) |
| *Maximum depth* | 200 m (656 ft) |
| *Torpedoes* | 14 |
| *Torpedo range* | 5,030 m (16,500 ft) |

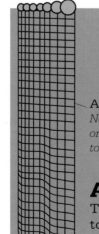

**Minefield**
*Mines were dropped from warships and planes. Magnetic ones were attracted to a U-boat's metal hull.*

**Depth charges**
*These were weapons dropped to explode at the estimated depth of a submarine.*

**Anti-submarine net**
*Nets were laid in harbours or around anchored ships to stop torpedoes.*

# Anti-U-boat measures
The Allies used powerful lights or radar to locate surface U-boats, and sonar to find them when they were underwater.

**U-boat defence**
*When under attack, U-boats fled or dived, then turned off their engines to stay quiet.*

**"The only thing that ever really frightened me during the war was the U-boat peril"** —WINSTON CHURCHILL

# Codes [Top secret]

Anyone can tune in to radio messages, so important ones were encrypted, or put into a code or cipher. The Allies' ability to break German and Japanese codes and ciphers gave them a vital advantage.

**Code**
Entire words or phrases are changed to new words, symbols, or letters.

**Original (plain text)**

**Cipher**
Each letter is changed. Here, letters have been moved ten places ahead in the alphabet.

## Cracking Enigma

The Germans invented a cipher machine called Enigma. They changed their ciphers daily and were convinced that they were unbreakable – but they were wrong. Helped by the Polish Cipher Bureau, the British cracked Enigma.

**Letter window**
*This showed the setting of each rotor when the cipher was changed.*

**Rotors**
*These changed each letter as it was typed in.*

**Keyboard**
*This was where the plain-text message was typed in, one letter at a time.*

**ALAN TURING**
Mathematician

Lived: 23 June 1912– 7 June 1954

Famous for: Building the first computer to help crack Enigma

**Bletchley Park**
The 2001 film *Enigma* was about Alan Turing and his team at Bletchley Park, England. They first cracked an Enigma message in 1940

## Tickertape secrets

Both sides used special teleprinters, which turned text into a cipher and printed it out as a set of punched holes on tape.

**1** A message is typed in plain text for a teleprinter machine to encrypt as a cipher.

**2** The machine punches holes into tickertape, which is fed into a special radio transmitter.

**3** The receiving teleprinter machine prints out the received encrypted message as punched tape.

**4** The message is deciphered using the same cipher settings, so it can be read as plain text.

**MESSAGE ENCRYPTED, READY TO SEND**

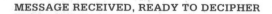

**MESSAGE RECEIVED, READY TO DECIPHER**

## Enigma
The machine needed two people to work it. One typed the message, one letter at a time. The other read out each new letter that lit up on the lampboard cover, as the plain text became a cipher to be sent.

**Lampboard cover**
*The letters here lit up to show the new encrypted message.*

**Plugboard**
*Wires here changed some of the letters again, making the cipher even more complicated.*

## Dots and dashes
Developed in the 19th century, Morse code represents the letters of the alphabet with sequences of dots and dashes. It was used throughout the war.

**MORSE SIGNALLING LAMP WITH GREEN AND RED FILTERS**

**TELEGRAPH KEY FOR SENDING MORSE ELECTRONICALLY**

### Sending Morse code
Signallers sent messages over long distances in the form of electronic pulses along telegraph wires, and over short distances as flashes of light.

## Japanese cipher
William F. Friedman of the US Signals Intelligence Service (SIS) looked for patterns in Japanese coded messages. Thanks to his work, the SIS cracked the Purple cipher in 1940. The Japanese never knew their security was breached.

**Wrecked plane**
In April 1943, top Japanese admiral Yamamoto Isoroku died after his plane was shot down. The USA had deciphered his travel plans.

## More here
*For key to symbols, see page 112*

**code** cipher **Purple cipher** Alan Turing **Enigma** **William F. Friedman**

***The Cracking Codebook: How to Make It, Break It, Hack It, Crack It*** by Simon Singh

***Mysterious Messages: A History of Codes and Ciphers*** by Gary Blackwood

***Enigma*** (2001) is based on the story of the Bletchley Park code-crackers.

**Bletchley Park** is a museum on the site of the British code-breaking centre and is home to the **National Museum of Computing**.

Visit the **National Cryptologic Museum**, in Fort Meade, Maryland, USA. Exhibits include a working German Enigma machine.

**Practise** writing messages in a shift cipher. Replace each letter with a letter a set number of places ahead in the alphabet.

# War i
# Pac

- Who masterminded the Pearl Harbor attack?

* Where did soldiers battle knee-deep in mud?

- What was so special about the B-24?

n the
ific

The Japanese captured territory in Southeast Asia, as well as many Pacific islands, before setting up defensive bases across the area. But their failure to knock out the US Navy turned the hope for new territory into a disaster as the US fought back.

## APR. 1942
## No rubber, no tyres
Japan's conquests gave it control of Asia's natural rubber, which deprived the United States of this vital material, used for tyres and other essential equipment. US scientists developed synthetic rubber from petroleum just before the natural rubber ran out.

US MILITARY JEEP

### YAMAMOTO ISOROKU
**Japanese navy**

| | |
|---|---|
| Lived: | 1884–1943 |
| Rank in 1941: | Commander of the Combined Fleet |

## DEC. 1941
## Pearl Harbor
Admiral Yamamoto planned Japan's surprise attack on the US Pacific Fleet's base at Pearl Harbor. It was meant to keep the USA from interfering with Japanese expansion. Four of the eight battleships in the harbour were sunk.

## 15 FEB. 1942
*Japan captured the British colony of Singapore.*

•1941                                                                                         194

**SEPT. 1940**
*Japan occupied French Indochina and became an ally of Germany and Italy.*

**JULY 1941**
*The USA and Britain blocked all trade with Japan, and the USA stopped supplying Japan with oil.*

**DEC. 1941**
*The USA declared war on Japan. Germany and Italy declared war on the USA.*

**DEC. 1941**
*Japan attacked Malaya and the Philippines to control the South China Sea.*

**9 APR. 1942**
*Japan captured the Philippines, preventing US planes from using it as a base.*

**JUNE 1942**
*The USA won the Battle of Midway, badly damaging the Japanese fleet.*

**AUG. 1942**
*US troops landed in the Solomon Islands.*

## MAR. 1942
## Internment
After the Pearl Harbor attack, 110,000 Japanese Americans living across the USA were forced to live behind barbed wire, in internment camps. Two-thirds were citizens born in the USA. Congress apologized for this in 1988.

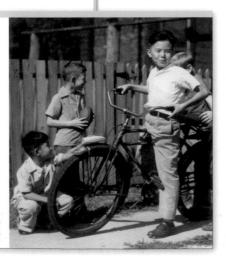

JAPANESE AMERICAN CHILDREN

## 18 APR. 1942
## Doolittle raid
The first US bomb attack on the Japanese capital, Tokyo, was planned and led by veteran pilot James "Jimmy" Doolittle. It did little damage, but this aerial return strike on Japan was a big victory for US morale and propaganda.

### JAMES DOOLITTLE
**US Air Force**

| | |
|---|---|
| Lived: | 1896–1993 |
| Rank in 1942: | Lieutenant colonel |

## MAY 1942
## Battle of the Coral Sea

US ships intercepted a Japanese fleet aiming to invade New Guinea and the Solomon Islands. For four days, each side sent planes to drop bombs and torpedoes. There was no outright winner, but Japan's losses were greater.

USS *LEXINGTON*, SINKING IN THE CORAL SEA

## 23–26 OCT. 1944
## Leyte Gulf

A series of massive battles was fought in the waters of Leyte Gulf, near the Philippines. The US victory cut off the supply route from mainland Japan to its forces in Southeast Asia, a plan masterminded by Admiral Nimitz.

### CHESTER NIMITZ
US Navy

| | |
|---|---|
| *Lived:* | 1885–1966 |
| *Rank in 1944:* | Commander in chief of the Pacific Fleet |

## JAN. 1943
*At the Casablanca Conference, Churchill and Roosevelt agreed that they should insist on unconditional surrender from the Axis powers.*

## NOV. 1943
*US landings on Bougainville, in the Solomon Islands, isolated Japanese forces and destroyed some of their key bases.*

## 19–20 JUNE 1944
*Japan lost 3 carriers and 426 of its 473 operational aircraft in the Battle of the Philippine Sea.*

*Dots represent yearly increases.*

## 12 APR. 1945
*President Roosevelt died and was replaced by his vice president, Harry S. Truman.*

•1944        •1945

## FEB. 1943
## War production

The US economy was set up for war. Car factories switched to building military vehicles. Millions of women joined the workforce, recruited by the newly created War Manpower Commission.

A RIVETER AT WORK ON A BOMBER IN A TEXAS FACTORY

## MAR. 1945
*A US air raid set Tokyo on fire. At least 83,000 people died, and 1.5 million lost their homes. US troops also captured Iwo Jima.*

## APR. 1944
## Battle of Imphal-Kohima

Battles at Imphal and Kohima, in India, turned back the Japanese invasion of Southeast Asia. Now Allied planes could fly from the area to attack the Japanese, who began to retreat through Burma.

CLEARING THE ROAD BETWEEN IMPHAL AND KOHIMA OF JAPANESE SOLDIERS

# 297,199:
## the number of military aircraft built in the United States during the war

# Pearl Harbor

On 7 December 1941, the Japanese attacked Pearl Harbor, on the Hawaiian island of Oahu. They hoped to wipe out the US Pacific Fleet, most of which was docked there. The surprise attack brought the United States into the war.

**6:10 AM** 183 planes took off from 6 Japanese aircraft carriers in the ocean 370 km (230 miles) north of the target. There were 51 dive-bombers, 49 bombers, 40 torpedo bombers, and 43 fighters.

**JAPANESE SAILORS WAVING OFF THEIR PLANES**

**7:45 AM** Dive-bombers attacked local airfields to give the Japanese control of the air. In all, 188 US planes were destroyed.

**7:53 AM** The Japanese aimed bombs and torpedoes at the 8 battleships anchored in the harbour.

**8:10 AM** The USS *Arizona* was hit by a bomb that ignited the gunpowder in its hold (cargo deck). In the ensuing explosion, 1,177 men died.

**8:54 AM** A second wave of 78 dive-bombers, 54 bombers, and 35 fighters arrived to attack the other 76 ships in the harbour, plus oil tanks and docks.

**9:55 AM** The second-wave planes returned to their carriers. They left behind 19 badly damaged or sunk ships – and a shocked nation. Comparatively few Japanese planes – 29 – were lost in the attack.

# 2,403
## Americans were killed in the attack on Pearl Harbor

# Culture during wartime

Both at home and on the front line, wartime music, radio shows, and movies expressed what people were fighting for and how much they missed their loved ones. People could escape their troubles for a while when they listened to a comedy on the radio or danced to the latest popular songs. Media had a more serious side, too, as governments everywhere used it to persuade citizens that their cause was right.

## Hollywood's leading role

Eager to forget the hardships of war, people flocked to cinemas to watch musicals and comedies. Hollywood helped the US government by producing films in which heroes fought evil invaders – the villains were nearly always German, Italian, or Japanese. Female characters in films were often shown doing their part as nurses or spies.

### Screen support
Like many movies of the time, *Casablanca* (1942) depicts Nazis as arrogant and members of the resistance as brave. It portrays the USA as a haven for the oppressed.

## Persuasion
Governments used propaganda (see page 17) at home to explain the war and encourage support for it. They also created propaganda to use against their enemies. Both sides tried to destroy their opponents' morale with radio broadcasts for enemy troops. An Allied tactic was to drop propaganda leaflets into occupied territory.

ENCOURAGING PEOPLE TO WORK AND FIGHT

THIRD WAR LOAN

RAISING MONEY FOR THE WAR EFFORT

BUILDING A SENSE OF NATIONAL IDENTITY

SHOWING THE ENEMY AS EVIL

# [Winning minds]

**Super sounds**
"Big band" groups performed jazz and swing on the radio and in dance halls. Pianist Duke Ellington's band was one of the most popular.

## All that jazz
Radio was how most people heard music, and it helped popularize jazz and swing. Hitler tried to ban jazz because of its links with African Americans and Jews, but many German troops listened to it.

## Boosting morale
The United Service Organizations (USO) put on up to 700 shows a day to keep up the spirits of US servicemen and women around the world. Stars of USO "camp shows" ranged from Laurel and Hardy to Lucille Ball. German troops had "front theatre" plays and cabarets.

**Zarah Leander**
Deep-voiced Swedish singer Zarah Leander was a superstar in Germany. She fled the country after her home was bombed in 1944.

**Hope for all**
Comedian Bob Hope was a huge attraction for the troops. In summer 1944, he island-hopped across the South Pacific to perform more than 150 shows, many of which were broadcast on live radio.

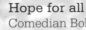

## More here
*For key to symbols, see page 112*

swing music jazz **jive**
USO **ENSA** "Lili Marlene"
**Glenn Miller** propaganda

*Propaganda*
by Charlie Samuels

***The Art of War: The Posters of World War II***
by Sean Price

*The Great Dictator* (1940), starring Charlie Chaplin, lampoons Hitler and his treatment of Jews.

Frank Capra's **Why We Fight** (1942–45) is a series of US propaganda films.

Disney's ***Der Fuehrer's Face*** (1942) features Donald Duck as a factory worker in Nazi Germany.

*49th Parallel* (1941) is about stranded U-boat sailors in Canada, trying to reach the still-neutral USA.

*Mrs Miniver* (1942) shows the effect of the war on a British housewife.

**"We're Going to Hang Out the Washing on the Siegfried Line"** is a comic British song about the German defensive line.

**"Rosie the Riveter"** is about a female assembly-line worker, who later also appeared on posters.

**"When the Atom Bomb Fell"** shows US attitudes at the end of the war.

**"GI Jive"**, by Johnny Mercer, was a hit jive song.

## Women and the war

These assembly-line workers are completing a B-17 bomber. During the war, the United States' female workforce rose from 12 to 18 million – there were similar increases in other fighting countries. Women took on everything from working on farms and driving buses and trains to operating radar, spying, and, of course, fighting. From 1945, millions of *Trümmerfrauen* ("rubble women") cleared Germany's wrecked cities brick by brick.

# Wartime childhood [Tough

War destroyed childhoods, as youngsters dealt with the losses of fathers, mothers, and homes. Everywhere, children struggled with shortages of food, clothes, and toys. Millions fled from battle zones or occupying armies. And millions more were killed by terrible bombings and in the Holocaust (see pages 42–45).

 **Germany**
In Germany, children aged 10–18 were expected to join Nazi youth organizations. Girls cared for the wounded in hospitals. Boys in the Hitler Youth were trained to help during air raids. They operated searchlights, fired anti-aircraft guns, and participated in the cleanup.

## Eyewitness
**NAME:** Emmy Werner

**DATE:** Born in 1929

**FROM:** Near Frankfurt, Germany

**DETAILS:** Emmy Werner was 10 years old when her country went to war. She later moved to the United States and became a psychologist.

**❝** I was 12 . . . and volunteered for the . . . air-raid watch. . . . We became experts at spotting incendiaries that had penetrated the roof of our schoolhouse or the classroom ceilings. Armed with buckets, we would race to throw sand over the eight-sided metal sticks before they exploded. **❞**

**Anti-aircraft gun**
From January 1943, boys in the Hitler Youth worked German anti-aircraft guns.

## Eyewitness
**NAME:** Shizue Kobayashi

**DATE:** Born in 1934

**FROM:** Saitama-ken, Japan

**DETAILS:** Shizue Kobayashi lived in Japan until she was 22 years old. In 1956, she emigrated to the United States to marry an airman who used to play baseball with the children at an orphanage she visited.

**❝** I wasn't allowed to eat as much as I wanted, just enough to keep me alive. After our potatoes were gone, we ate weeds we found in the yard. We were lucky, though, because a lot of people were dying of hunger. **❞**

 **Japan**
Bombings and food shortages forced many Japanese families to move from the cities to the countryside. The most nimble-fingered girls worked in factories, making fire balloons – bomb-carrying hydrogen balloons that were launched toward the United States and Canada.

## United States

American children helped the war effort by collecting newspapers, rubber tyres, and tin cans for recycling. In the month of October 1942, 30 million children collected 1.5 million tonnes of scrap metal for producing aircraft and munitions.

### Eyewitness

**NAME:** Joan Dooley

**DATE:** 1942

**FROM:** Wichita, Kansas, USA

**DETAILS:** Joan Dooley was a 12-year-old Girl Scout when she wrote to General Douglas MacArthur, supreme commander of the southwest Pacific war.

❝ My mother saves grease for bullets. I also buy a war stamp every time I get a quarter. We save paper, all kinds of metal and rubber. I have a bicycle but I don't very often ride it to save rubber tyres. . . . We Girl Scouts are doing our bit by taking care of small children so that the parents may work in war factories.❞

BUY WAR BONDS

THIRD WAR LOAN

**War bonds**
Even children were encouraged to buy war bonds, which raised money for the war effort.

## Britain

In Britain, hundreds of thousands of children were evacuated from bomb-threatened cities to the safer but unfamiliar countryside. Sweets were rationed, along with other foods, and any treats were highly prized. Children swapped old toys and books and wished for new, war-themed books about tanks, battleships, or warplanes.

### Eyewitness

**NAME:** Jean Bruce

**DATE:** Born in 1935

**FROM:** Manchester, England

**DETAILS:** Jean Bruce was 3 years old when the war started, but she remembers the air raids, rationing, and her Mickey Mouse gas mask. She later emigrated to Canada.

❝ People had to queue up for everything (though rationing made things fairer). Sometimes Mum would see a queue forming and join it, not even knowing what was for sale at that shop. One orange was a very rare treat carefully shared out segment by segment, and I didn't have a banana throughout the war. ❞

**Ruined Berlin**
For children in cities across Europe, the daily walk to school became a trek across a bomb site.

**A night out**
To escape air raids, families crammed into cold, damp shelters (like this reconstruction) in their gardens.

## More here

*For key to symbols, see page 112*

*Remember World War II: Kids Who Survived Tell Their Stories* by Dorinda Makanaonalani Nicholson

*Rosie the Riveter: Women in World War II* by Sean Stewart Price

*The Machine Gunners* by Robert Westall

*Goodnight Mister Tom* (1999) and *Carrie's War* (2006) are both adapted from books about evacuated children.

Look out for reruns or the DVDs of *Hogan's Heroes*, a comedy series about POWs in wartime Germany.

"Any Bonds Today?," sung by the singing trio the Andrews Sisters, encouraged people to help fund the war by buying government war bonds.

"We'll Meet Again," by the English performer Vera Lynn, was a sentimental song about soldiers leaving their families behind.

Experience the sights, sounds, and smells of the Blitz, and step inside an air-raid shelter at the **Imperial War Museum London**.

Explore the home front gallery and theatre at the **Wright Museum of WWII History**, in Wolfeboro, New Hampshire, USA.

# Sea battles [Pacific turning-

By early 1942, Japan was victorious throughout the Pacific and Southeast Asia, so it needed to defend the supply routes to these conquests against attacks by the Allied fleet. The Pacific became a war zone, where submarines, warships, and aircraft carriers battled.

**MAP KEY**
- Japanese territory
- Allied territory

Battle of Midway

Extent of Japanese control, July 1942

Battle of the Coral Sea

MANCHURIA · JAPAN · CHINA · BURMA · PHILIPPINES · THAILAND · NEW GUINEA · AUSTRALIA

## Battle of the Coral Sea

In May 1942, Japan and the USA engaged in a battle in the Coral Sea. The ships involved never saw or fired on one another. Instead, each side used an aircraft carrier to launch bombers to attack the enemy fleet. After four days, the result was a costly draw.

| Battle of the Coral Sea: losses | USA | Japan |
| --- | --- | --- |
| Aircraft carriers | 1 | 1 |
| Warships | 1 | 4 |
| Oil tankers | 1 | 0 |
| Aircraft | 66 | 77 |
| Men | 654 | 1,074 |

### Reasons for war
The Battles of the Coral Sea and Midway were both fought to keep Japan from capturing more bases in the Pacific.

# Battle of Midway

Japan planned to draw out the US fleet with a decoy attack on the Aleutian Islands. On 4 June 1942, one force would ambush the US carriers off Midway Island while another conquered Midway itself. However, the USA had cracked Japan's coded messages. It hit the Japanese with waves of torpedoes and dive-bombers. Midway was a turning-point in the Pacific war. Japan never recovered from its losses.

| Battle of Midway: losses | USA | Japan |
| --- | --- | --- |
| Aircraft carriers | 1 | 4 |
| Warships | 1 | 1 |
| Aircraft | 132 | 275 |
| Men | 307 | 3,507 |

### Doomed aircraft carrier

Allied planes were launched from USS *Yorktown*. The carrier was damaged at Coral Sea and sunk just after the Battle of Midway.

## 1 Aleutian attack

The decoy strike was to allow Admiral Nagumo to destroy the US fleets while Admiral Yamamoto conquered Midway.

ALEUTIAN ISLANDS

JAPAN

Admiral Nagumo's fleet
Admiral Yamamoto's fleet

Task force 17 *(including USS* Yorktown*)*

Japan's planned attack routes

MIDWAY

Area under US submarine surveillance

Task force 16 *(including USS* Enterprise *and* Hornet*)*

HAWAIIAN ISLANDS

## 2 Early draw

The first waves of Japanese and US planes set off at almost the same time. Neither side managed to deliver a knockout blow to its target.

180° W
179° W
178° W
177° W

Nagumo's fleet of four carriers
*Soryu*
*Akagi*
*Hiryu*
*Kaga*

7 AM
*Bombers took off from US carriers.*

USS *Enterprise*
USS *Hornet*

47 of the 51 US torpedo planes shot down

USS *Yorktown*

4:30 AM
*Japanese bombers took off to attack Midway.*

4:45–6:00 AM
*US bombers took off from Midway Island.*

30° N

## 3 US success

While the Japanese fought off one wave of US attackers, another US group got through and hit three carriers.

Hit
*Akagi, Soryu, and Kaga sank.*

12 PM
*USS* Yorktown *was hit.*

11 AM
*Dive-bombers were launched from Hiryu.*

### Backup

*Planes from USS* Hornet *headed to protect Midway Island.*

8:30 AM
*All three US carriers launched planes to attack Nagumo's fleet.*

## 4 Massive defeat

*Hiryu* launched planes at USS *Yorktown* before it sank. Admiral Yamamoto's approaching fleet had to retreat.

June 5
*Hiryu sank.*

5:05 PM
*Hiryu was severely hit.*

2:40 PM
*USS* Yorktown *was badly hit.*

1:30 PM
*Torpedo bombers were launched from Hiryu.*

3:30 PM
*USS* Enterprise *launched dive-bombers to attack Hiryu.*

**MAP KEY**

- US Task force 17
- US Task force 16
- Japanese fleets

From December 1941, Japan invaded many Pacific islands, as well as Asian countries such as Malaya and Burma. It quickly learned how to fight in the dense jungle. Now US, British, Australian, and other Allied troops had to do the same. This fighting was up close and nasty, as small groups crawled on their bellies or waded through swamps.

## Under attack

Enemies could be lurking above or below ground – but they were only one of the dangers soldiers faced in the jungle. Troops on both sides feared mosquito bites, which could transmit deadly malaria or dengue fever.

**Jungle worries**
For every 1 combat casualty, Allied doctors treated as many as 100 soldiers suffering from heatstroke or tropical diseases.

**Extreme heat**
*Temperatures could soar to 38°C (100°F), causing exhaustion and dehydration.*

**Bad water**
*Micro-organisms in dirty water led to dysentery, cholera, and typhoid.*

**Venomous snakes**
*Vipers could kill with a single bite.*

**Malaria**
*This disease caused fever, convulsions, and death.*

**Dengue fever**
*This virus led to fever, rashes, and even death.*

**Tall grass**
*Razor-sharp kunai grass cut through flesh like a knife.*

**Leeches**
*These bloodsuckers left wounds that could soon become infected.*

**Jungle rot**
*Tropical ulcers formed on the skin and rotted away the flesh.*

## Eyewitness

**NAME:** George Henry Johnston

**DATE:** 1942

**FROM:** Melbourne, Australia

**DETAILS:** Johnston (1912–70) was a war correspondent for the *Melbourne Argus* newspaper.

" Churned up by the troops of both armies, the track itself is now knee-deep in thick black mud. For the last ten days no man's clothing has been dry, and all have slept when sleep was possible in pouring rain under sodden blankets. Each man carries his personal equipment, firearms, ammunition supply, and five days' rations. Every hour is a nightmare. "

**Mud march**
In November 1943, US marines headed to Bougainville Island, part of New Guinea, to confront the Japanese.

# 80%

## of US soldiers in some South Pacific units were infected with malaria

## Japanese tactics

Japanese snipers lashed themselves to trees or hid in dugouts in order to surprise the enemy, particularly at night. They would call out in English to trick Allies in the dark, and they always fought to the death.

**Dugout**
*The main bunker could house a small detachment of troops.*

**Crawl trench**
*These tunnels connected the dugout to the foxholes.*

**Foxhole**
*One-man gun pits radiated out from the main dugout.*

**Dugout walls**
*Bamboo or corrugated iron strengthened the walls.*

**Fire!**
*The sniper or machine gunner fired through a slit in the wall.*

**Hideout**
Both sides used dugouts like this one to rest in between patrols or as bases for surprise sniper attacks.

**Camouflage**
*Earth, brushwood, or leaves hid the whole complex from sight.*

## Holdouts

Japanese troops were trained not to give up. Some, left behind in remote areas, never heard that the war was over. These soldiers stayed in their jungle dugouts for years, or even decades, because no one had ordered them to leave.

**Holdout Hiroo Onoda surrenders**
Officer Hiroo Onoda was 52 when he handed over his sword, dagger, rifle, and hand grenades in 1974. He had hidden in the Philippines for nearly 30 years.

# Guns [Weapons of war]

During the war, gun technology improved. At first, soldiers put up with outdated models. Later, they were armed with new, state-of-the-art weapons that had faster firing rates and greater accuracy, and were less likely to jam or overheat.

TOKAREV TT-33 HANDGUN, SOVIET

COLT M1911 PISTOL, US

SMITH & WESSON REVOLVER, BRITISH

SVT-40 RIFLE, SOVIET

LEE-ENFIELD MK III RIFLE, BRITISH

M1 CARBINE RIFLE, US

STEN SUBMACHINE GUN, BRITISH

PPSH-41 SUBMACHINE GUN, SOVIET

THOMPSON SUBMACHINE GUN, US

BOYS ANTI-TANK RIFLE, BRITISH

DEGTYAREV DP MACHINE GUN, SOVIET

ROCKET LAUNCHER, BRITISH

BREN MACHINE GUN, BRITISH

VICKERS MEDIUM MACHINE GUN, BRITISH

## Types of gun

**Handgun**
Most officers carried a revolver or automatic pistol. Allied soldiers prized the sleek German Luger P08 as a war souvenir.

**Rifle**
Most rifles needed reloading after each shot, so the US semi-automatic M1 Carbine was a technological revolution.

**Automatic rifle**
The Germans were the first to make an accurate, quick-firing, self-loading assault rifle, the Gewehr 41(W).

TYPE 14
PISTOL,
JAPANESE

BROWNING HI-POWER
HANDGUN, GERMAN

MAUSER C96
HANDGUN, GERMAN

MAUSER KAR98K RIFLE, GERMAN

MP40
SUBMACHINE
GUN, GERMAN

CARCANO M91 RIFLE, ITALIAN

TYPE 38 RIFLE,
JAPANESE

LUGER P08
HANDGUN,
GERMAN

BERETTA MODEL 38
SUBMACHINE GUN,
ITALIAN

TYPE 99 MACHINE GUN,
JAPANESE

PZB 39 ANTI-TANK
RIFLE, GERMAN

STG44 (ALSO KNOWN
AS MP43 AND MP44)
AUTOMATIC RIFLE, GERMAN

MG42 MACHINE GUN, GERMAN

### Submachine gun
These shot 400 to 800 rounds per minute in short bursts. Top performers were the German MP40 and the US Thompson.

### Machine gun
Each section of eight to ten men had support from a lightweight machine gun. Heavy machine guns, usually tripod-mounted, were better for long-range targets.

### Anti-tank weapon
In 1942, the US Army invented the rocket-firing bazooka, a weapon that can penetrate thick tank armour.

# POWs [Incarcerated]

All sides held POWs, or prisoners of war – captured soldiers, airmen, and sailors – in camps to prevent them from fighting again. In countries that had signed the Geneva Conventions, such as Britain and the United States, POWs were mostly treated well. In the Soviet Union and Japan, they were starved and beaten.

**International parcels**
Some fortunate POWs received Red Cross packages containing treats such as butter, biscuits, chocolate, and dried food.

## Camps in the West

POW camps were set up all over Europe and the United States. Prisoners occupied themselves by making crafts, reading, and learning new skills. Sometimes they worked on local farms or built roads and waterways. For most, it was a boring but safe wait for the war to end.

**Field work**
POWs in Britain could not escape their island prison, and many were trusted to work on farms.

### Eyewitness

**NAME:** Janina Skrzynska
**POW:** Dec. 1944–Apr. 1945
**FROM:** Poland
**DETAILS:** Skrzynska was in the Polish Home Army; she was captured by the Nazis after the Warsaw Uprising. She was held in a women's camp at Oberlangen, Germany.

" One barrack was used as a chapel, while two more were left empty. These we exploited as an extra supply of fuel: we took out planks from the bunks, pulled up floorboards. . . . In the mornings and evenings [we had] a tepid herbal tea, . . . mouldy bread, the occasional piece of margarine, or a spoonful of beetroot marmalade. At midday, . . . soup from bitter cabbage or grubby peas with two or three jacket potatoes. "

**Colditz Castle**
This fortress near Dresden, Germany, was for POWs whose escapes had failed. The war ended before they could fly the glider they had built in the attic!

## Great escapes

Allied POWs in Germany made many escape attempts. Their efforts ranged from making fake guard uniforms and simply walking out, to digging tunnels to get beyond the fences. Of the 76 who tried this one night from Stalag Luft III, 3 made it back to Britain, 23 were returned to the camp, and 50 were shot on Hitler's orders.

## Camps in the East

Life for prisoners in Japanese POW camps was extremely harsh. POWs were fed tiny amounts of rice. Beatings were common, and POWs were forced to work in mines or on a railway between Burma and Thailand.

**March of death**
In April 1942, the Japanese marched captured soldiers 135 km (85 miles) in six days to a camp. They beat or killed those who fell – 10,000 Filipinos and 650 Americans died.

### Eyewitness

**NAME:** Thomas Arthur Craigg, Jr
**DATE:** Born 20 January 1918
**POW: 6** May 1942–26 Aug. 1945
**FROM:** Arkansas, USA
**DETAILS:** Gunnery Sergeant Craigg was wounded in action on 2 May 1942, at Corregidor, while defending the Philippines. He was taken prisoner by the Japanese and transported in a "hell ship" to Japan, where he was forced to work in coal mines 12 hours a day.

❝ We was on one ration a day of rice. That ration of rice didn't amount to much more than a coffee-cup full of rice. But that's what we had to eat for some time. And it wasn't long until things begin to taper off a little bit, not so many people dying. The stronger had survived and we was put on working details, whatever the Japanese had for us to do. Some of us went out to help repair bridges. Some details left and went back to the air force field that we had there and do repair work on that. And others would go and do repair work on bridges, on roads. ❞

# 60,000
**Allied POWs were forced to help build the Burma Railway;**
## one in five died

**Changi prisoners**
Changi was a notoriously tough Japanese POW camp in Singapore, where inmates had a simple choice – work or starve.

## More here

*For key to symbols, see page 112*

***Prisoner of War***
by Stewart Ross
***Life as a POW***
by John F. Wukovits

***The Great Escape*** (1963) is an exciting film based on true stories of Allied POW escapes.
***The Colditz Story*** (1955) is about the many attempted escapes from this fortress.

The **Aliceville POW Museum**, in Alabama, USA, has drawings and objects made by German POWs.

**Geneva Conventions:** a series of articles that describe how injured soldiers and POWs should be treated. The first convention was introduced in 1864. Japan and the Soviet Union did not sign the 1929 convention.

**hell ship:** a Japanese ship carrying Allied POWs crammed into the holds, with little to eat or drink.

**Polish Home Army:** a resistance movement in Poland that fought against Nazi and Soviet occupation.

**Red Cross:** an international organization founded in Switzerland in 1863 to help victims of conflict. It sent 36 million aid parcels during the war.

**stalag:** a German POW camp. The largest, Stalag VII-A, held 130,000 Allied soldiers.

# B-24 [Long-range bomber]

More B-24 Liberators were built than any other US military plane. This long-range bomber flew faster and farther than other planes, and with heavier loads. But it burned quickly if its fuel tanks were hit, so it was nicknamed the "flying coffin".

**18 hours:** the time taken to build each B-24 Liberator

**Building B-24s**
Ford's Willow Run plant, near Detroit, USA, was built for making B-24s. The assembly line was 1.6 km (1 mile) long.

**Oxygen bottles**
*Spare oxygen was for the crew to breathe.*

## All-arounder
The B-24 was far more than just a heavy bomber. It could attack submarines and ships, lay mines, transport people and supplies, and carry out photographic reconnaissance missions and weather checks.

**Top gun turret**
*The plane's engineer manned the gun in this Plexiglas turret.*

**Cockpit crew**
*B-24 pilots needed strength to handle the heavy controls.*

**Nose turret**
*This protective turret had a shield of bulletproof Plexiglas.*

**Bomb bay doors**
*The doors rolled back into the fuselage to keep the plane streamlined.*

**Bombs away!**
*Most B-24s carried ten 227 kg (500 lbs) bombs, or five 454 kg (1,000 lbs) ones.*

**Machine guns**
*These .50-calibre guns could fire 800 rounds a minute.*

**Electric heaters**
*Heaters kept the guns from freezing in the cold, high air.*

**Nose wheel**
*This prevented the plane from tipping when on the ground.*

250551

## Bomb types

The versatile B-24 carried crater-making general-purpose bombs and fire-starting cluster bombs. Other missiles included radio-guided ones for tricky targets, and torpedoes for dropping in water.

**GENERAL-PURPOSE BOMB**
AN-M64: 227 KG (500 LBS)

**INCENDIARY CLUSTER BOMB**
AN-M17A1: 227 KG (500 LBS)

**RADIO-GUIDED BOMB**
VB-1 AZON: 454 KG (1,000 LBS)

### Tail gun turret
*This could swing 180 degrees for fast fighting.*

### Stabilizer
*Twin tails helped keep the plane more stable while in the air.*

### Camera mount
*This held the camera used for reconnaissance.*

### Fuselage
*The flat-sided, boxy fuselage allowed maximum cargo space.*

### Waist gun position
*Gunners working in the waist (another name for the fuselage) also released tinfoil, called chaff, to confuse enemy radar.*

### Ball turret
*This gun turret could turn in a full circle. It tucked into the fuselage during landings and takeoffs.*

### Retractable wheel
*The two main wheels used on the ground folded into the wings during flight.*

### Turbocharged
*Four air-cooled, 1,200-horsepower engines powered the B-24.*

### Davis wing
*Clever shaping enabled the wings to lift the plane with its heavy loads.*

| B-24 specifications | |
|---|---|
| Introduced | 1941 |
| Number made | 18,482 |
| Crew members | 8–10 |
| Length | 20.6 m (67 ft 8 ins) |
| Weight (empty) | 116,556 kg (36,500 lbs) |
| Wingspan | 33.5 m (110 ft) |
| Range | 3,380 km (2,100 miles) |
| Top speed | 467 kph (290 mph) |
| Guns | 10 machine guns (sometimes 11) |
| Bomb cargo (short range) | 3,600 kg (8,000 lbs) |
| Bomb cargo (long range) | 2,300 kg (5,000 lbs) |

Jungle warfare through Southeast Asia was slow and deadly. The Allies needed a different strategy against the Japanese. From June 1943, they began to conquer islands around powerful Japanese bases. As the Allies gained control of sea and air, they were able to keep supplies from reaching enemy troops. This leapfrogging to the next target en route to Japan itself was called island-hopping.

*MANCHURIA*

*KOREA*

*Sea of Japan*

*JAPAN*

*East China Sea*

Okinawa
*June 1945*

**4** **End of the line**
The advancing Allied lines met at Okinawa, which became their base for air attacks on Japan.

Iwo Jima
*Feb.–Mar. 1945*

*CHINA*

**3** **Leyte Gulf**
In October 1944, Japan counter-attacked in the Battle of Leyte Gulf. Much of its fleet was destroyed.

*BURMA*

*South China Sea*

*PHILIPPINES*

*Philippine Sea*
*June 1944*

## Kamikaze killers

The Japanese adopted a terrifying new tactic in October 1944 at the Battle of Leyte Gulf – kamikaze, or "divine wind", attacks. Pilots flew bomb-filled planes straight into targets. By the end of the war, the Japanese had carried out about 2,800 of these suicide missions.

Leyte Gulf
*Oct. 1944*

**PALAU ISLANDS**

Peleliu
*Sept.–Nov. 1944*

Mindanao

Morotai
*Sept. 1944*

*DUTCH BORNEO*

### In for the kill
A kamikaze fighter plane hurtles toward the USS *Missouri*, off Okinawa, in April 1945. The battleship survived the attack.

*NEW GUINEA*

*Banda Sea*

*JAVA*

*Timor Sea*

## The fleet train

Supplies are vital in any war. To fight in the Pacific, US troops, ships, and aircraft had to be fed, fuelled, and armed 8,000 km (5,000 miles) away from the US mainland. The solution was the fleet train, a convoy of tankers and other ships that could replenish supplies at sea.

**TYPES OF SHIP IN A CONVOY**

**DESTROYER**

**ESCORT CARRIER**

**CARGO SHIP**

**TROOP TRANSPORTER**

**MUNITIONS SHIP**

**GASOLINE TANKER**

**OIL TANKER**

**HOSPITAL SHIP**

## Attack ships

Destroyers and escort carriers were ready to attack Japanese submarines, ships, or planes that came too close.

## Supply ships

Tankers and ships carried massive stocks of the chilled and dried foods, fresh water, fuel, and munitions needed to fight a war.

# 1.5 million
**Japanese servicemen died in the Pacific War, compared to 103,000 US troops**

Route of Allied attack fleet, led by Admiral Nimitz from the naval base at Pearl Harbor

**Pearl Harbor**
**HAWAIIAN ISLANDS**

Saipan
*July 1944*

Tinian
*July 1944*

Guam
*July 1944*

Enewetak
*Feb. 1944*

Kwajalein
*Feb. 1944*

**MARSHALL ISLANDS**

**GILBERT ISLANDS**

## Pacific progress

The Allies' ultimate target was the Japanese mainland. In 1942, a series of sea battles, especially the Battle of Midway (see page 65), weakened Japan's navy and air force. Then, in June 1943, Operation Cartwheel began – the island-hopping strategy to isolate Japan's Pacific bases.

**CHUUK ISLANDS**
*Japan's major Pacific base*

**2** Leapfrogging
From 1943, the Allies encircled key Japanese strongholds, such as the massive Chuuk Lagoon base and the southern base at Rabaul.

Admiralty Islands
*Feb.–May 1944*

Tarawa
*Nov. 1943*

Rabaul
*Japanese base*

Bougainville
*Nov. 1943*

**SOLOMON ISLANDS**

Guadalcanal
*Aug. 1942–Feb. 1943*

Route of Allied attack fleet, led by General MacArthur from the naval base at Brisbane, Australia

**1** Two lines of attack
There were two prongs to the fight. One went across the central Pacific (blue line), the other across the southwest Pacific (yellow line).

**MAP KEY**

- - - Extent of Japanese control, July 1942
▪ Japanese territory
▫ Allied territory
✶ Allied victory

# The Battle of Iwo Jima

Iwo Jima is a tiny Pacific island 1,100 km (700 miles) from Japan's capital, Tokyo. Allied planes needed to use its airstrips for attacks on the Japanese mainland. It was a key target.

As many as 21,000 Japanese defenders on Iwo Jima dug bunkers connected by 18 km (11 miles) of tunnels. On 19 February 1945, they watched 30,000 US marines land on the beaches, then started firing. When the fierce fighting ended five weeks later, only 212 Japanese remained alive. Japan's unshakable willingness to fight to the end led the United States towards its decision to drop atomic bombs and end the war.

# War in A
# & the Mid

* Which German general was known as the Desert Fox?

* What dangers did tank commanders face?

* How did the Allies win their victory at El Alamein?

frica
lle East

# Africa and the Middle East

For 32 months, starting from September 1940, Allied and Axis forces battled back and forth in North and East Africa. This was a deadly game of chess played across the hot desert with tanks, artillery, and troops. The prize was access to Middle Eastern oil.

## APR. 1941
## The siege of Tobruk

Rommel's forces surrounded and bombarded Tobruk, trapping 14,000 Australians. Fighting back from a defensive network of trenches and tunnels, the Australian troops nicknamed themselves "the rats of Tobruk".

GERMAN TROOPS AND TANKS NEAR TOBRUK

## JULY 1940
## Naval attack

The British wanted to keep the Germans from taking control of the French fleet in the Algerian port of Mers El Kébir. They attacked, sinking three battleships.

BATTLESHIPS ON FIRE AT MERS EL KÉBIR, ALGERIA

### JAN. 1941
*Allied forces swept on from Egypt to take the key port of Tobruk, in Libya.*

### DEC. 1941
*The Allies forced Rommel's army away from Tobruk to relieve the siege.*

**1941**        **1942**

*Dots represent yearly increases.*

### 10 JUNE 1940
*Italy declared war on Britain and France. Mussolini had 300,000 Italian and African troops based in Libya.*

### JULY 1940
*In East Africa, Italy attacked the British colonies of Sudan and Kenya.*

### DEC. 1940
*British troops, numbering 36,000, defeated a force of 75,000 Italians in Egypt.*

### 27 NOV. 1941
*Italian forces lost a key battle at Gondar, Abyssinia (now Ethiopia), with the surrender of 23,500 men. Italy was finally forced out of East Africa.*

# 85,000
# litres (22,195 gallons): the amount of fuel the Afrika Korps needed every week

**ERWIN ROMMEL**
German army

| | |
|---|---|
| In Africa: | Feb. 1941–May 1943 |
| Rank in 1941: | General |
| Nickname: | The Desert Fox |

## FEB. 1941
## The Afrika Korps

German forces, battle-hardened from their successes in Europe, arrived to support the struggling Italians. The German Afrika Korps was led by Rommel, an experienced and clever general.

# [Desert warfare]

## 1–27 JULY 1942
## First Battle of El Alamein

The small Egyptian town was the last line of Allied defence before the Suez Canal. Allies and Germans battled to a draw that weakened Rommel's over-extended army.

A BRITISH 14-CM (5.5-INS) ARTILLERY GUN USED AT EL ALAMEIN

## 10 JULY 1943
## Invasion of Sicily

It took a total of 450,000 Allied soldiers 38 days to drive retreating Italian and German troops from the island of Sicily in the Mediterranean Sea. For this mission, codenamed Operation Husky, Allied troops arrived by boat and by parachute.

BRITISH TROOPS LANDING ON SICILY

### 8–14 NOV. 1942
*To the east, in Operation Torch, the Allies landed in French North Africa.*

### JAN. 1943
*The British took Tripoli, in Libya, forcing the Axis armies back east into Tunisia.*

### 8 SEPT. 1943
*Italy surrendered. Allied troops had invaded five days earlier, and they kept advancing from the south.*

**1943**          **1944**

### MAY 1942
*Rommel's attack at Gazala, Libya, pushed the Allies back into Egypt.*

### 21 JUNE 1942
*The German Afrika Korps captured Tobruk and 35,000 Allied troops.*

### AUG. 1942
*The first of 300 US Sherman tanks arrived in North Africa. They were to prove vital.*

### 19–25 FEB. 1943
*The Battle of Kasserine Pass was Rommel's last victory, as his forces beat the newly arrived US troops.*

### MAY 1943
*With hardly any supplies left, Axis forces surrendered in Tunisia.*

### 13 OCT. 1943
*Italy switched sides and declared war on Germany, its former ally.*

## AUG. 1942
## Troop morale

General Bernard Montgomery took command of the British Eighth Army. He made speeches directly to his troops, explaining how he planned to defeat Rommel. This made him very popular.

### BERNARD MONTGOMERY

**British army**

| | |
|---|---|
| In Africa: | Aug. 1942 – May 1943 |
| Rank in 1942: | General |
| Nickname: | Monty |

## 23 OCT.–4 NOV. 1942
## Second Battle of El Alamein

Montgomery used rubber tanks, wooden trucks, and dummy railways to deceive the Germans. His victory at El Alamein marked the point at which Rommel began his retreat.

AN INFLATABLE RUBBER DECOY TANK

# War in the desert [Sand

War came to North Africa in September 1940, when Italy used its African colony Libya as the base for an advance on British-occupied Egypt. Mussolini's ultimate target was the crucial Suez Canal. When the Allies pushed the Italians back, Hitler sent his Afrika Korps to the fight. Now the desert war raged.

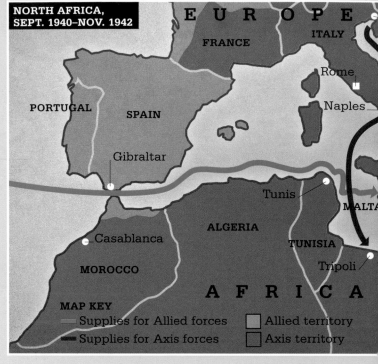

**NORTH AFRICA, SEPT. 1940–NOV. 1942**

EUROPE
FRANCE
ITALY
Rome
Naples
PORTUGAL
SPAIN
Gibraltar
Tunis
MALTA
Casablanca
ALGERIA
TUNISIA
MOROCCO
Tripoli
AFRICA

MAP KEY
— Supplies for Allied forces  ☐ Allied territory
═ Supplies for Axis forces  ☐ Axis territory

## Combined forces
Thousands of Australians and New Zealanders, known as ANZACs, fought in Africa alongside soldiers from India, South Africa, and all over the British empire. During July 1942 and again in October, they fought the Germans for control of El Alamein, Egypt.

**Digging trenches**
In August 1942, these New Zealanders dug trenches to defend the patch of desert that they had won at the First Battle of El Alamein.

## Supply routes
Resources were scarce in this undeveloped territory, much of which was desert, so both sides had to bring all their supplies. Tobruk was a major prize because it was the port nearest to the front lines, where the armies needed food, fuel, and ammunition in vast quantities.

**Into Africa**
Allied supplies came along the Suez Canal or through the British territory Gibraltar. Axis supplies sailed into Tripoli, then trucked along the coast road.

## Fighting team
Hitler created his Afrika Korps in February 1941, selecting his popular commander Erwin Rommel to lead it. Rommel used the Wehrmacht's fast, surprise blitzkrieg methods (see pages 22–23) brilliantly.

**Minefields**
Millions of mines were hidden just below the sand, primed to blow up if tanks drove over them.

**Moving at night**
Troop movements across the open desert took place at night, under cover of darkness.

## Desert tactics
Both sides often began attacks with blasts of artillery. Then the infantry would advance, supported by tanks. It was important to stay within reach of supplies, or fuel-hungry tanks might be stranded. Spies provided intelligence about where the other side was and where it was going.

**Decoy tanks**
Tanks dragged metal chains to create clouds of dust that looked like an army on the move.

**Poisoning water**
If troops retreated, they poisoned water supplies to keep this vital resource from the enemy.

### Sun goggles
Goggles blocked the sun and the windblown sand. Rommel had a favourite pair, which he captured from a British officer.

## Hard times
Desert conditions were tough. The days were blisteringly hot but the nights were cold. Vehicles and shellfire whipped up sandstorms, and the grit turned the tiniest scratches into painful sores. Food spoiled in the heat, dysentery was common, and water was too scarce to waste on washing.

### Medical care
Casualties were treated at field hospitals. The use of penicillin and blood transfusions saved millions of lives.

## Eyewitness

**NAME:** Hans Klein

**DATE:** Born in 1921

**FROM:** Germany

**DETAILS:** Klein was a furniture-maker before he joined the German forces. He served as a private in the Afrika Korps from 1942 to 1943 and was awarded the Iron Cross medal for bravery.

❝ Flies were a problem, and we had no control over them. Nets that we wore over our faces at all times protected us from the flies and allowed us to enjoy eating. To eat some bread with jelly, first you had to get all the flies off the bread and then quickly slip it under your net – hoping not to bring them all inside the net with you. ❞

### Popular leader
Rommel (far left) inspired great respect from his troops. He lived, ate, and fought alongside his men, and cared for their welfare.

# M4 Sherman [Fast and nasty]

The United States shipped the first M4 tanks to North Africa in the late summer of 1942. At last the Allies had a fast-moving, fast-firing tank with the power to punch holes in German armoured vehicles. The M4 was used in all theatres of war. The British called the newcomer the Sherman after the famous Civil War general.

**On track**
More M4s were made than any other tank. Mass-produced at 11 different factories, they were used by British, Canadian, and Free French forces, as well as by the US military.

## Hot and noisy

The tank's crew members had to cope with the sweltering heat and deafening roar of the engine and gun, using hand signals to communicate. Early Shermans caught fire easily when fired on, so crews reinforced the armour with extra metal sheets, timber, or sandbags. If they were hit, they scrambled out of an escape hatch underneath the vehicle.

Gunner
*Second in command, this gunner operated the turret gun.*

75-mm (3-in) gun
*The gun fired shells that could penetrate more than 6 cm (2.5 ins) of armour.*

Driver's hatch
*The driver's seat was raised so that he could look through this hatch when not under fire.*

Browning machine gun
*The twin .30-calibre machine guns came with 6,250 rounds of ammunition.*

Hull machine gunner
*This gunner was also the tank's co-driver and radio operator.*

Driver's control levers
*Levers were linked to the left and right tracks, which turned the tank.*

## Stopping a tank

In an attempt to halt these apparently unstoppable monsters, anti-tank guns fired armour-piercing shells or grenades, and land mines were planted ahead of an expected advance. In close-up battles, enemy soldiers dropped grenades inside the tanks.

M24 GRENADE

ANTI-TANK MINE

PZB 39 ANTI-TANK RIFLE

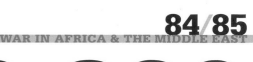

**Tank commander**
*He gave directions to the driver and chose targets for the gunners.*

**Turret casing**
*The iron turret was cast in one 7.5-cm (3-in) thick piece for maximum strength.*

# 49,230

## Shermans were built – it was the main tank used by the Allies in World War II

**Ammunition loader**
*His job was to take shells from the ammunition rack and load the turret gun by hand.*

**Turret**
*The electric motor–driven turret could turn in a full circle, unlike the turrets of other tanks.*

**Armour plating**
*This was 5 cm (2 ins) thick on the sides, but only 6 mm (0.25 ins) on top.*

**Engine**
*The gasoline-fuelled, 400-horsepower engine was tilted to fit into the tank's shell.*

**Ammunition**
*The tank carried 90 rounds of 75-mm (3-in) shells.*

**Drive shaft**
*The propeller shaft connected to the front-mounted transmission.*

**Wheels**
*Each track ran on 12 lower, 4 upper, and 2 rear wheels.*

**Suspension**
*A spring suspension system absorbed some of the bumps on rough ground.*

**Track**
*The 42-cm (16.5-in) wide rubber tracks each had 79 "shoes".*

| M4A1 specifications | |
|---|---|
| Introduced | 1941 |
| Number made | 49,230 |
| Crew members | 5 |
| Weight (empty) | 30.3 tonnes |
| Length | 5.8 m (19 ft 2 ins) |
| Width | 2.6 m (8 ft 7 ins) |
| Height | 2.5 m (8 ft 2 ins) |
| Range | 193 km (120 miles) |
| Top speed | 45 kph (28 mph) |
| Fuel capacity | 796 litres (210 gallons) |
| Turret gun | 75 mm (3 ins) |

# Spies and special ops

The most dangerous wartime missions were behind enemy lines. Spies risked their lives learning about troop movements, weapons development, and other sensitive information. Special forces attacked key targets such as supply lines.

## Special ops

All sides had special operations (ops) units. Their operatives were trained in close combat so that they could kill an enemy guard in a prison or munitions factory without the noise of a gun raising an alarm.

### Special Air Service
The British SAS was formed in July 1941 to attack behind German lines in North Africa. In one early mission, an SAS force blew up 60 German aircraft without a single British casualty.

### Scouts and Raiders
Formed in the USA in 1942, the Scouts and Raiders specialized in underwater reconnaissance. Many of their missions involved supporting troop landings.

## Spy rings

All countries had intelligence agencies and spies. Many spies worked in counter-espionage, or stopping enemy spies. Some were double agents who passed on false information.

### US OSS
The Office of Strategic Services was the USA's first spy agency, its staff trained by the British secret services. It ran spy networks around the world and later became the CIA.

| | |
|---|---|
| Founded: | 1942 |
| Operatives: | 24,000 |
| Known for: | Spying in Nazi Germany; supporting partisans against Japan |

### SPY: VIRGINIA HALL
US agent Hall worked in Vichy France for the SOE and then the OSS. She found sites where weapons for resistance fighters could be dropped, helped airmen who had been shot down escape, and reported on German troop movements. She was nicknamed "the Limping Lady" because of her wooden foot, the result of a hunting accident. Hall died in 1982 at age 76.

### British SOE
The Special Operations Executive supported resistance movements in Europe and Asia. Its agents were trained in creating disguises, parachuting, weapons usage, unarmed combat, map reading, and radio communications.

| | |
|---|---|
| Founded: | July 1940 |
| Operatives: | 13,000 |
| Known for: | Helping resistance movements; feeding fake information to the Germans |

### SPY: JOAN PUJOL GARCIA
Spanish-born Garcia persuaded the Germans to take him on as a spy – but only because he wanted to work as a double agent. His sympathies lay with the British. Garcia gave the Germans fake information about D-Day, convincing them that the landings would take place further up the coast. After the war, Garcia faked his own death and went to live in Venezuela.

### German Abwehr
The Abwehr was the Wehrmacht's military intelligence bureau, loyal to Germany, not to Hitler. It was involved in an attempt on Hitler's life in 1944. The SD, a rival intelligence agency, reported to high-ranking Nazi Heinrich Himmler.

| | |
|---|---|
| Founded: | 1921 |
| Operatives: | Number unknown |
| Known for: | Infiltrating a Dutch underground unit |

### SPY: ELYESA BAZNA
Bazna worked for the British ambassador in Turkey, but he was really a German spy, with the codename Cicero. Whenever the ambassador took a bath, Bazna opened a safe and photographed secret documents. The British later claimed that Bazna was a double agent. Doublecross became triplecross after the war when Bazna realized that the Abwehr had paid him with counterfeit money.

## Soviet GRU

Stalin did not trust anyone, so spies from the GRU, the main Soviet intelligence agency, infiltrated both Allied and Axis powers. GRU agents uncovered German battle plans that proved crucial in winning the Battle of Kursk in July 1943.

| | |
|---|---|
| *Founded:* | 1921 |
| *Operatives:* | Thousands (exact number unknown) |
| *Known for:* | Stealing information on the atomic bomb |

## SPY: RICHARD SORGE

Sorge was a German Communist who supported the Soviet Union. He worked as a journalist in Germany, where he joined the Nazi Party as part of his cover. He warned Stalin about Hitler's invasion plans in 1941 but was ignored. Sorge then ran a spy network in Japan but was discovered by the Japanese and hanged in 1944. He has been called the greatest spy of all time.

## Japanese spies

In Japan, all agents studied the martial art of aikido. Some learned Russian so that they could spy in the Soviet Union. Others scouted Pearl Harbor before the 1941 attack. Many aided local nationalists in Asia, who wanted freedom from western colonial rule.

| | |
|---|---|
| *Founded:* | 1938 |
| *Operatives:* | 2,500 |
| *Known for:* | Finding weaknesses in Singapore's defences |

## SPY: VELVALEE DICKINSON

US-born Dickinson ran a doll-trading business in New York – but she was also a spy. Writing to an address in Argentina, she sold information to the Japanese. Her letters, intercepted by the FBI, seemed to be about dolls but were in code and actually detailed US naval ship repairs and movements. In 1944, Dickinson was found guilty of espionage and sentenced to ten years in jail.

# Spy kit

Secret agents used a range of equipment, from simple to of the latest technology. Their spy gear had to be easy to carry and conceal, but quick to bring out and use.

**Garrote**
*This length of wire, used to strangle victims, could retract into the handle.*

**Concealed knife**
*The 13.5-cm (5.5-ins) blade was released by a button on the handle.*

**Cudgel**
*The weighted steel ball could be used to club someone on the head.*

## Multipurpose weapon

The McLaglen Peskett close-combat weapon was three weapons in one: a garrote (strangle wire), a knife, and a cudgel. Just 18 cm (7 ins) long, it was very easy to hide on the body, perhaps strapped to a leg.

**Hidden blade**
Blades were hidden in many ways – inside heels of shoes, fake coins, or, in this case, an innocent-looking pencil. Blades were useful for cutting tyres or wires, as well as people.

**Pencil**
*The wood has been cut away to reveal the blade inside.*

**Silencer**
*The silencer muffled the bang of the gun.*

## Modified Luger

This silenced Luger pistol was part of the kit intended to be used in the attempt to assassinate Hitler on 20 July 1944.

**Sure shot**
This tiny camera, about 9 cm (3.5 ins) across, was seized from a spy after the war. Light, small, and easy to conceal, it could take pictures of documents at close range.

# Victory in North Africa

The turning-point of the war took place in North Africa. In late 1942, General Montgomery led the Allied forces across the desert. The Second Battle of El Alamein shocked Germany into retreat for the first time. Then, as British and US forces poured in, the African coast became the launchpad for an invasion of Italy that brought the battle back into Europe.

**African trap**
After the Allied triumph at El Alamein, Allied forces stormed ashore in Morocco and Algeria, trapping Rommel in Tunisia. The surrounded Axis forces surrendered on 13 May 1943.

**MAP KEY**
— Allied fleet
— UK troops
— German troops

## Second Battle of El Alamein

**SEPT.– OCT. 1942**
Rommel laid 3 million mines across the front, in two 8-km (5-mile) belts. To trick Rommel about his tank positions, Montgomery placed dummy tanks to the south and disguised real tanks as trucks.

**23 OCT.**
After a six-hour artillery barrage, the Allies advanced at night.

**24 OCT.**
Montgomery's troops slowly cleared paths through the minefields for their advancing columns of tanks.

**25 OCT.**
To the north, Australian troops captured a key German lookout post, Point 29.

**26 OCT.**
British bombers sank a German oil tanker in the Mediterranean, off Tobruk, Libya, adding to Rommel's supply problems.

**2 NOV.**
After a seven-hour artillery barrage, the Allies advanced, punching a 19-km (12-mile) wide hole in the German lines.

**3 NOV.**
The advancing Allies found enemy forces ready to surrender or already gone. The Germans left behind thousands of vehicles with empty fuel tanks.

**9 NOV.**
Rommel's forces lost a key position at Sidi Barrani, in northwestern Egypt.

**11 NOV.**
Despite Hitler's orders to stand and fight, the Axis forces retreated from Egypt. 25,000 had been killed or wounded, and a further 25,000 had been captured. The Allies suffered just 13,000 casualties.

> **"The battle is going very heavily against us. We're being crushed by the enemy weight"**
> —ERWIN ROMMEL, 3 NOVEMBER 1942

**14 CM (5.5 INS) ARTILLERY GUN, BRITISH**

### The crunch
Fought mostly at night, across a 64-km (40-mile) long front in the Egyptian desert, the Second Battle of El Alamein halted the Axis advance toward the Middle East and sent the Germans into retreat. Having cracked German codes, the Allies knew that Rommel was ill and short on fuel. His 110,000 troops and 559 tanks were outnumbered by the Allies' 195,000 men and 1,351 tanks, including the new US Shermans.

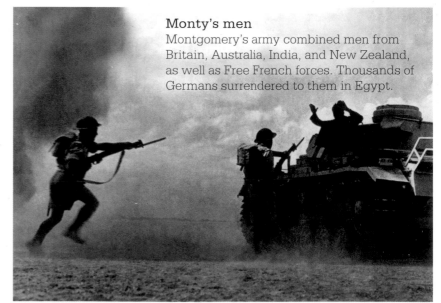

**Monty's men**
Montgomery's army combined men from Britain, Australia, India, and New Zealand, as well as Free French forces. Thousands of Germans surrendered to them in Egypt.

## Sicily and beyond

The Allies gathered a huge invasion force to cross the Mediterranean, and they began by attacking the island of Sicily. The Germans were not prepared, because they had found a planted body, floating in the sea off Spain, that carried plans of fake invasions. Sicily was captured in August 1943. The Allies invaded Italy on 3 September, and Italy surrendered five days later. Germany fought on.

**Over the waves**
At dawn on 10 July 1943, a fleet of 2,590 ships transported 180,000 troops to the eastern and southwestern coasts of Sicily. In all, 450,000 Allied troops landed during the 38-day battle.

# 60,000:
## the number of casualties suffered by both sides at Monte Cassino

## Battle of Monte Cassino

Occupied by German forces, the historic hilltop monastery of Monte Cassino, Italy, blocked the Allies' route north from southern Italy to Rome. The Allies attacked on 17 January 1944, but German troops were able to hold out until 18 May.

**A town in ruins**
Intensive bombing and shelling wrecked Monte Cassino and the town below. Craters and rubble made perfect foxholes for the German defenders.

# The
# of th

- On which famous day did the Allies invade France?

* What happened after Germany surrendered?

- How did one Little Boy flatten a whole city?

# end
# e war

As the Allies pushed Nazi forces back to Berlin, some of the bloodiest battles of the war in Europe were fought. In the Pacific, Japan resisted stubbornly until the dropping of two atomic bombs forced its surrender.

## FEB. 1945
## Yalta

The heads of Britain, the USA, and the Soviet Union met at the city of Yalta, in the Crimea (now Ukraine). They agreed to divide Germany into zones and to form the United Nations (UN), and Stalin promised to declare war on Japan.

**CHURCHILL, ROOSEVELT, AND STALIN AT YALTA**

**DWIGHT EISENHOWER**
**US Army**

| | |
|---|---|
| Lived: | 1890–1969 |
| Rank in 1944: | Supreme commander of Allied forces in Europe |
| Nickname: | Ike |

## 6 JUNE 1944
## D-Day

General Eisenhower landed the first of 2 million Allied troops on five beaches in Normandy, France, ready to push back the Germans. The invasion involved 4,000 landing craft, 1,200 warships, and 14,500 planes.

**27 JAN. 1944**
*At last, the survivors in the besieged Soviet city of Leningrad were freed.*

**13 JUNE 1944**
*The first German V-1 flying bombs landed in England. Each "doodlebug" carried a 848-kg (1,870-lbs) warhead.*

**8 SEPT. 1944**
*Germany targeted London with the first V-2 rockets.*

• **1944** •

**JULY–AUG. 1943**
*At Kursk, in the Soviet Union, the Soviets defeated the Germans in the largest tank battle ever. There were 6,500 tanks in the battle.*

**NOV. 1943**
*Meeting in Tehran, Iran, Roosevelt and Churchill promised Stalin that they would invade France the following May.*

*Dots represent monthly increases.*

## 16 DEC. 1944
## Final push

In a last-ditch offensive, the Germans attacked the Allies in northern France, making the Allies' front line bulge inwards. The Battle of the Bulge lasted six weeks, but under Patton's leadership, the Germans were pushed back.

**GEORGE PATTON**
**US Army**

| | |
|---|---|
| Lived: | 1885–1945 |
| Rank in 1944: | General |
| Nickname: | Old Blood and Guts |

## 25 AUG. 1944
## Paris freed

General Dietrich von Choltitz surrendered Paris to the Allies. He had disobeyed Hitler's orders to destroy its monuments and bridges. The Allies arranged for a French-led division to march in to reclaim the capital city.

**A VICTORY PARADE IN PARIS**

# 19,000:
## the number of US soldiers who died in the Battle of the Bulge

## 13–15 FEB. 1945
### Dresden bombing
British and US bombers dropped high explosives and firebombs on the previously untouched city of Dresden, Germany. The fires were so hot that they created 145 kph (90 mph) winds, and the roads melted. About 25,000 people died.

B-17 FLYING FORTRESS

# 316:
## the number of
# Flying
## Fortresses
## that flew in the
## raids over
## Dresden

## 14 AUG. 1945
### Japan surrenders
Following massive US bombing raids on Tokyo from 10 to 14 August, Emperor Hirohito announced Japan's surrender. The official surrender ceremony took place on 2 September.

THE SURRENDER CEREMONY

## 7 MAY 1945
*In Reims, France, General Alfred Jodl surrendered German forces to the Allies.*

## 26 JULY 1945
*The USA, Britain, and China told Japan to surrender or face "utter destruction".*

## 6 AUG. 1945
*A US uranium bomb destroyed the Japanese city of Hiroshima.*

## 24 OCT. 1945
*The United Nations was founded with the aim of building world peace.*

## 24 MAR. 1945
*Allied forces crossed the Rhine River and advanced into the heart of Germany.*

**1945** — **1946**

## 17 JAN. 1945
*Soviet forces captured the Polish capital, Warsaw, and freed it from German rule.*

## 28 APR. 1945
*Mussolini was captured and shot, along with 13 others, by Italian partisans.*

## 2 MAY 1945
*After a week of street fighting, the Red Army took control of Berlin.*

## NOV. 1945
*A series of trials began in Nuremberg, Germany, to try Nazi leaders for war crimes.*

## 30 APR. 1945
### Hitler's suicide
As the Red Army advanced on Berlin, Hitler shot himself in the underground air-raid bunker complex that had been his home since January. Hours before he died, he married Eva Braun, who also committed suicide.

A BRITISH NEWSPAPER REPORTING HITLER'S DEATH

## 9 AUG. 1945
### Nagasaki
The US dropped a 6.4-kg (14-lbs) plutonium bomb on the Japanese port city of Nagasaki. The explosion killed at least 40,000 people, with tens of thousands more dying in the weeks and months that followed.

THE MUSHROOM CLOUD ABOVE NAGASAKI

## D-Day

At dawn on 6 June 1944, Allied troops landed in France to start the attack on Hitler's armies across Europe. This was the scene on Omaha Beach, one of five landing points along a 80-km (50-miles) stretch of the Normandy coast. More than 158,000 men landed on D-Day itself, the first of a total invasion force of 2 million.

## More here
*For key to symbols, see page 112*

**D-Day** Omaha Beach
Dwight Eisenhower
**Utah Beach**

***D-Day Landings:*** *The Story
of the Allied Invasion*
by Richard Platt

***Remember D-Day:*** *The
Plan, the Invasion,
Survivor Stories*
by Ronald J. Drez

***D-Day Remembered*** is
a documentary about the
Normandy landings, with
eyewitness accounts.

***Ike: Countdown to D-Day***
focuses on the planning
of the invasion by General
Dwight Eisenhower.

Visit the **landing beaches**
along the Normandy
coastline. There are **D-Day
museums** in Ouistreham
and Arromanches, France.

The **D-Day Museum** in
Portsmouth includes the
Overlord Embroidery,
a tapestry tribute to the
troops involved in D-Day.

**D-Day:** a military term
short for *day day* – the
chosen day for a particular
event. Specifically, *D-Day*
now refers to 6 June 1944.

# Battle of the Bulge [Nazi

At the end of 1944, the Allied advance eastwards across Europe towards Berlin seemed inevitable. Then, in December, the Germans launched a surprise attack that became known as the Battle of the Bulge. This offensive held up the advance for two months.

## Still operational

The Allies destroyed the massive bunkers that were the secret launch sites for Germany's V-2 rockets. But the Nazis continued to launch V-2s from mobile units.

**Deadly rockets**
Through the winter of 1944–45, around 2,500 people in London alone were killed by V-2s, many of which were launched from country roads in northern Europe.

## Stretched thin

The Allies' advance across war-ravaged Europe was filled with difficulties and terrors. The Germans had left mines and booby traps. Snipers hid in ruined buildings. The Allied commanders stretched their lines thin – the 130-km (80-miles) front in the Ardennes, between Belgium and France, was held by 60,000 US troops. When the Germans attacked, they did so with 200,000 men.

**Slow progress**
Soldiers had to use mine detectors to clear buildings that the retreating Germans had booby-trapped.

**Icy warfare**
Allied soldiers were forced to fight against almost overwhelming odds in the thick forests and narrow valleys of the Ardennes, in gruelling weather. Here, a US Seventh Armoured Division patrols the Belgian village of Saint Vith.

## Into battle

Hitler wanted to split the British, Canadian, and US armies in the Ardennes, and block a key supply route. The US forces were pushed back, but Allied counterattacks and German fuel shortages ended the battle after six weeks.

### The "bulge"

This map shows the bulge created by the advance of 200,000 German soldiers. They found a weak point in the Allied lines.

**6** 25 January
*Weeks of counterattacks forced the Germans to halt the assault.*

**5** 23 December
*Better weather allowed Allied planes to fly 15,000 trips in 4 days to attack troops and supply lines.*

**4** December 21
*German troops surrounded and besieged Bastogne, trapping 18,000 US troops.*

BELGIUM
Malmédy
Dinant
ARDENNES
GERMANY
Bastogne
FRANCE
LUXEMBOURG

**1** 16 December
*The Germans bombarded the Allies. Bad weather prevented a response.*

**2** 17 December
*German forces pushed both north and south.*

**3** 19 December
*The Germans had now created a bulge in the Allied lines.*

### Battle of the Bulge: losses

|  | Allied | German |
|---|---|---|
| *Dead* | 20,876 | 15,652 |
| *Casualties* | 42,893 | 41,600 |
| *Captured or missing* | 23,554 | 27,582 |

### MAP KEY

| | |
|---|---|
| — Allied troops | — front line 16 Dec. |
| — German troops | ···· front line 20 Dec. |
| Allied territory | -- front line 25 Dec. |
| German territory | |

## Eyewitness

**NAME:** Robert C. Cable

**DATE:** 1944

**LOCATION:** Belgium

**DETAILS:** From Cleveland, Ohio, Cable was a 19-year-old soldier in the US Army's Seventeenth Airborne Division. He described the Battle of the Bulge as "the worst Christmas I ever spent".

"The weather conditions were atrocious. We were losing 2,000 men a day, not to combat so much as to the weather. I mean frozen feet, frozen fingers, everything. We had a lot of problems with that."

# Berlin falls [Victory in Europe]

In 1945, as Allied forces advanced on Berlin from east and west, Hitler stayed in his bunker. Stalin was determined to crush the German capital, so the other Allies held back as 2.5 million Red Army troops entered the city. The war in Europe was over, but in the Pacific and Asia, it continued for three more months.

## Fall of Berlin

The Russians encircled Berlin and then captured it street by street. Out for revenge, they looted shops and robbed civilians. After Hitler's suicide, German generals eventually had no choice but to surrender.

**Soviet advance**
On 30 April 1945, Red Army tanks rumbled toward the Reichstag, the German parliamentary building.

## Eyewitness

**NAME:** Dorothea von Schwanenfluegel

**DATE:** 20 April 1945

**DETAILS:** Polish-born Schwanenfluegel moved to Germany as a child. In 1945, she was a 29-year-old mother in Berlin.

❝ We noticed a sad-looking young boy across the street, standing behind some bushes in a self-dug, shallow trench. I went over to him and found a mere child in a uniform many sizes too large for him, with an anti-tank grenade lying beside him. Tears were running down his face, and he was obviously very frightened. . . . [H]e had been ordered to lie in wait here, and when a Soviet tank approached, he was to run under it and explode the grenade. ❞

## Fall of Berlin: Timeline

**16 Apr.** *The Soviets began to bombard Berlin's outer defences. German deserters were hanged from the trees.*

**20 Apr.** *Hitler celebrated his birthday by decorating Hitler Youth boys with medals. The last Anglo-US air raid on Berlin took place.*

**26 Apr.** *The Soviets had control of the suburbs. Marshals Zhukov and Konev were competing to claim Berlin.*

**30 Apr.** *The battle for the Reichstag began. Hitler and his wife committed suicide. Joseph Goebbels was made chancellor.*

**Tea for victory**
At this celebratory tea party in London, children ate sandwiches and cake at a giant V-shaped table.

## Victory and defeat

War-weary civilians and troops from Allied countries celebrated Victory in Europe (V-E) Day with street parties and dancing. But in German and Italian cities, people starved, as did many others in wartorn lands. Across Europe, 12 million refugees began the long journey home.

### Eyewitness

**NAME:** Mollie Panter-Downes

**DATE:** 19 May 1945

**DETAILS:** Born in August 1906, Panter-Downes was an English novelist who wrote the Letter from London column for the *New Yorker* magazine.

❝ The government decided against sounding the sirens in a triumphant 'all clear', for fear that the noise would revive too many painful memories. For the same reason, there were no salutes of guns – only the pealing of the bells, and the whistles of tugs on the Thames sounding the doot, doot, doot, dooooot of the 'V', and the roar of the planes, which swooped back and forth over the city, dropping red and green signals towards the blur of smiling, upturned faces. ❞

**US celebrations**
Jubilant crowds gathered in cities across the USA, especially New York. They marked V-E Day with tickertape parades, cheering, singing, and triumphant flag-waving.

**1 May** *Goebbels and his wife committed suicide after poisoning their six children. Admiral Dönitz became head of Germany.*

**2 May** *General Weidling, in charge of Berlin's defences, surrendered the city on the radio, saying: "Anyone who falls for Berlin dies in vain."*

**4–5 May** *Thousands of German troops marched west to surrender to British and US forces rather than to the Soviets.*

**8 May** *V-E Day: The Germans officially signed their surrender in Berlin, with Soviet, US, British, and French witnesses.*

## Hiroshima

The Pacific war dragged on, and in the summer of 1945, the United States decided to force Japan to surrender by deploying a devastating new weapon – the atomic bomb. Its first target was the city of Hiroshima. When the Japanese did not surrender right away, a second bomb was dropped, on the city of Nagasaki. These powerful weapons produced blistering heat that killed instantly, and deadly radiation that caused death and suffering for years afterwards.

**6 AUG.**

**THE ATOMIC BOMB LITTLE BOY**

**2:45 AM** The B-29 bomber *Enola Gay* took off from the Pacific island of Tinian. Its deadly cargo was "Little Boy", the atomic bomb destined for Hiroshima.

**8:15 AM** Little Boy was dropped on Hiroshima, a city of 300,000 people. A fireball 600 m (2,000 ft) in diameter engulfed everything. At least 70,000 people died instantly.

**8:25 AM** The mushroom cloud billowed up to a height of 12,190 m (40,000 ft).

**9 AUG.** The atomic bomb "Fat Man" was detonated over Nagasaki. The blast killed at least 40,000 people.

**15 AUG.** Emperor Hirohito announced on the radio that Japan would surrender.

**6 SEPT.** After a month, 70,000 more citizens of Hiroshima had died from burns or radiation sickness.

## "The enemy has begun to employ a new, most cruel bomb"
—EMPEROR HIROHITO'S SURRENDER SPEECH

# The war in numbers

World War II was the biggest and most terrible war the world has ever seen. There were 61 countries involved, and 1.9 billion of their populations took up arms and fought. About 1 in every 40 people in the world died, many of them civilians. The war lasted so long because Germany and Japan stubbornly fought on even when it was clear that they could not win.

## WWII in context

When US president Woodrow Wilson took the United States into World War I in 1917, he called it "a war to end all wars". These casualty statistics show that, sadly, he was wrong.

### Different styles

Previous wars were fought by armies charging at one another and fighting hand to hand. World War II was far more destructive.

**WORLD WAR II**
1939–1945
69,700,000

**WORLD WAR I**
1914–1918
15,000,000

**RUSSIAN CIVIL WAR**
1917–1922
9,000,000

**THIRTY YEARS' WAR**
1618–1648
7,000,000

**NAPOLEONIC WARS**
1799–1815
4,000,000

**CHINESE CIVIL WAR**
1927–1950
3,000,000

**ENGLISH CIVIL WAR**
1642–1651
868,000

**AMERICAN CIVIL WAR**
1861–1865
620,000

**SPANISH CIVIL WAR**
1936–1939
500,000

**KEY**
= 1 million dead

## World War II lasted

# 2,174 days

## War machine

The fighting on land, at sea, and in the air called for the production of enormous amounts of extra equipment. Factories in the United States supplied much of the Allied armoury. They employed mass-production techniques and recruited 3 million women to work in special war factories, which tremendously boosted the workforce.

### Decades of debt

These are some of the pieces of equipment shipped from US factories during World War II. The Allies took decades to pay back their debts.

**650,000 jeeps**

**300,000 aircraft**

**89,000 tanks**

**2,751 cargo ships to Britain**

**3,000,000 machine guns**

**14,000,000 pairs of boots to Russia**

## Horse sense

Horses were still important for transportation. Troops rode them, and they hauled artillery and other equipment on muddy and snowy routes that overwhelmed wheeled vehicles.

**RUSSIA**

**GERMANY**

**FRANCE**

**KEY**
= 1 million horses

### At the front line

On the eastern front, most German artillery and supplies were horse-drawn, and the Soviets had cavalry units.

# [Fatal facts]

## War dead

Why did 2.5 percent of the world's population die? Death rates soared when large regions, such as the Soviet Union and China, were invaded. Many Holocaust victims came from eastern European countries, while in divided nations, such as Yugoslavia, partisans fought one another.

**KEY**
**MILITARY CASUALTIES**
**CIVILIAN CASUALTIES**

### FULL WIDTH = 10,000,000 CASUALTIES

**SOVIET UNION:** MILITARY 9,750,000 • CIVILIAN 13,650,000 • TOTAL 23,400,000

**CHINA:** MILITARY 3,500,000 • CIVILIAN 11,500,000 • TOTAL 15,000,000

**GERMANY:** MILITARY 5,527,000 • CIVILIAN 2,175,000 • TOTAL 7,702,000

**POLAND:** MILITARY 240,000 • CIVILIAN 5,480,000 • TOTAL 5,720,000

**DUTCH EAST INDIES (INDONESIA):** MILITARY 0 • CIVILIAN 3,500,000 • TOTAL 3,500,000

**JAPAN:** MILITARY 2,120,000 • CIVILIAN 750,000 • TOTAL 2,870,000

**INDIA (BRITISH):** MILITARY 87,000 • CIVILIAN 2,000,000 • TOTAL 2,087,000

**YUGOSLAVIA:** MILITARY 373,000 • CIVILIAN 990,000 • TOTAL 1,363,000

**FRENCH INDOCHINA (VIETNAM):** MILITARY 0 • CIVILIAN 1,125,000 • TOTAL 1,125,000

### FULL WIDTH = 1,000,000 CASUALTIES

**PHILIPPINES:** MILITARY 57,000 • CIVILIAN 750,000 • TOTAL 807,000

**ROMANIA:** MILITARY 300,000 • CIVILIAN 500,000 • TOTAL 800,000

**HUNGARY:** MILITARY 300,000 • CIVILIAN 280,000 • TOTAL 580,000

**FRANCE:** MILITARY 217,600 • CIVILIAN 350,000 • TOTAL 567,600

**GREECE:** MILITARY 27,550 • CIVILIAN 535,000 • TOTAL 562,550

**ITALY:** MILITARY 301,400 • CIVILIAN 155,600 • TOTAL 457,000

**UNITED KINGDOM:** MILITARY 383,800 • CIVILIAN 67,100 • TOTAL 450,900

**KOREA (JAPANESE):** MILITARY 0 • CIVILIAN 430,500 • TOTAL 430,500

**UNITED STATES:** MILITARY 416,800 • CIVILIAN 1,700 • TOTAL 418,500

**AUSTRIA:** MILITARY 260,000 • CIVILIAN 120,000 • TOTAL 380,000

**CZECHOSLOVAKIA:** MILITARY 25,000 • CIVILIAN 300,000 • TOTAL 325,000

**NETHERLANDS:** MILITARY 17,000 • CIVILIAN 284,000 • TOTAL 301,000

**BURMA:** MILITARY 22,000 • CIVILIAN 250,000 • TOTAL 272,000

**ABYSSINIA (ETHIOPIA):** MILITARY 5,000 • CIVILIAN 95,000 • TOTAL 100,000

**MALAYA (BRITISH):** MILITARY 0 • CIVILIAN 100,000 • TOTAL 100,000

**FINLAND:** MILITARY 95,000 • CIVILIAN 2,000 • TOTAL 97,000

**BELGIUM:** MILITARY 12,100 • CIVILIAN 75,900 • TOTAL 88,000

**SINGAPORE (BRITISH):** MILITARY 0 • CIVILIAN 50,000 • TOTAL 50,000

**CANADA:** MILITARY 45,400 • CIVILIAN 0 • TOTAL 45,400

**AUSTRALIA:** MILITARY 39,800 • CIVILIAN 700 • TOTAL 40,500

**NEW ZEALAND:** MILITARY 11,900 • CIVILIAN 0 • TOTAL 11,900

**SOUTH AFRICA:** MILITARY 11,900 • CIVILIAN 0 • TOTAL 11,900

### Civilian fatalities

The huge numbers of non-combatants killed during the war include the victims of genocide. Millions also died from starvation, city bombings, or revenge killings after invasions.

There was 1 death every **3** seconds throughout the war

The war ended, but suffering did not. Cities and towns were flattened, food was scarce, and millions had lost their homes. For people all over the world, recovery took decades. New countries and alliances formed, and the whole way the world was organized changed radically.

## Postwar Europe

Stalin took control of Eastern Europe and the Baltic States to create a new Soviet-controlled empire. The USA and the Soviet Union were the new "superpowers", but they did not get along. Their strained relationship was known as the Cold War; it became more dangerous, starting in 1949 when the Soviets made an atomic bomb.

**Different ideologies**
From 1948, Europe was split into two blocs – the Communist East and the democratic, capitalist West. Each of the Eastern European states had a Communist government that was loyal to the USSR.

**MAP KEY**
■ Under Soviet control

**A new nation**
The Declaration of Independence of the State of Israel was made on 14 May in Tel Aviv.

## State of Israel

The newly formed United Nations decided that Jews should have their own country. In May 1948, in a controversial move, it created the state of Israel by splitting the region of Palestine into Arab and Jewish states. Hundreds of thousands of surviving European Jews flooded in to help create the "Promised Land". Some Arabs in the region had to move out.

**Divided city**
By the late 1940s, Berlin, surrounded by Communist East Germany, was divided into the Communist East and the democratic West. The Berlin Wall literally divided the city between 1961 and 1989.

## Home for heroes

Millions of soldiers returned home – by 1947, the number of armed forces from the United States alone shrank from 12 to 1.5 million. Many soldiers found it difficult to adjust to civilian life.

# 40 million:
## the number of refugees in Europe when the war ended

**Welcome home!**
The *Queen Mary* docked in New York on 20 June 1945, carrying 15,642 troops, including 7,000 Canadians. About 435,000 GIs arrived home every month for the next year.

**Hostile actions**
The superpowers raced to develop deadly weapons. The US tested the first H-bomb in November 1952. The Soviet Union matched it in 1953.

## Towards peace

In the war's aftermath, world leaders tried to safeguard against such a terrible conflict ever happening again. They also focused on rebuilding war-torn countries' shattered economies.

**OCT. 1945**

On 24 October, 51 countries formed the United Nations, an international organization aimed at avoiding future wars and supporting basic human rights around the world.

**NOV. 1945**

On 20 November, the Nuremberg Trials began and 22 Nazi leaders were charged with war crimes before an international war tribunal. Of these, 12 were sentenced to death, and others were imprisoned.

## The postwar world

With the major European nations weakened or needing aid after the war, countries that had been colonies left their European rulers or were encouraged to become independent. The age of empires was over. Communism gained influence as the balance of world power changed.

### Berlin conquered
The Red Army entered Berlin on 21 April 1945. They looted buildings and attacked many civilians in revenge for the devastation caused by the Nazis.

### China turns Communist
In 1949, Mao Tse-tung won a three-year civil war and largely isolated China until 1976.

### Independent India
Mahatma Gandhi's Quit India campaign helped end British rule in August 1947. India and the new state of Pakistan became independent.

### Changes in Japan
The Japanese emperor lost all political and military power in 1947. Japanese women voted for the first time in the 1948 elections.

**1947**

The American Marshall Plan pumped $13 billion into European countries to support industry and agriculture.

**1949**

On 4 April, Western powers fearful of Communist threats formed the North Atlantic Treaty Organization (NATO), a political and military peacekeeping alliance.

**1951**

The European Coal and Steel Community, a stepping stone to the European Union, was founded to join countries in an economic union and to make war less likely.

**aircraft carrier**
A large warship with a long, open deck from which aircraft can take off and on which they can land while at sea.

**air raid**
An attack by military aircraft, usually large groups of bombers.

**air-raid shelter**
A structure to protect people during air raids. This might be a cellar, a tunnel, an Anderson shelter in the garden, or an underground station.

**Allied forces**
The 26 nations that fought against the Axis powers in World War II. Members included Great Britain, the Soviet Union, the USA, Canada, France, and China.

**anti-Semitism**
Hatred of the Jewish people, often leading to persecution.

**appeasement**
The act of making undue concessions to satisfy the demands of someone greedy for power.

**Aryan**
To the Nazis, a white, non-Jewish person. A pure Aryan had blond hair and blue eyes.

**atomic bomb**
A nuclear weapon that releases a huge amount of energy. It creates an enormous explosion and spreads harmful radiation.

**Axis powers**
In World War II, Nazi Germany, Fascist Italy, and Japan. Their alliance began in 1936 and lasted until their defeat in 1945.

**blackout**
A period of darkness in a city during an air raid (achieved by turning off or hiding all lights), to make it harder for enemy aircraft to find their targets.

**Blackshirt**
An armed member of a Fascist group founded in Italy by Benito Mussolini in 1919. Blackshirts were named for their uniforms.

**Blitz**
The devastating night-time bombings of Britain and Northern Ireland by the German Luftwaffe from September 1940 to May 1941. The main targets were large cities and ports.

**blitzkrieg**
A military manoeuvre in which the attacking army moves fast and is supported by tanks and aircraft. *Blitzkrieg* is a German word meaning "lightning war".

**chaff**
Thousands of tiny strips of tinfoil, dropped from planes to produce a confusing image on enemy radar screens. This made incoming planes hard to spot.

**cipher**
A way of hiding the meaning of a message by changing its letters.

**civilian**
Someone who is not on active duty in the armed services.

**colony**
A country or region ruled by another country.

**Communism**
A set of beliefs about how society should be run, based on the idea that everyone should be treated the same and all property should be shared.

**concentration camp**
A large guarded compound where civilians, especially Jews, were kept in very harsh conditions. In some camps, also known as extermination or death camps, the prisoners were deliberately killed.

**convoy**
A fleet of ships or group of vehicles traveling together, often protected by an escort of warships or armed troops.

**D-Day**
A military term short for *day day* – the chosen day for a particular event. Specifically, *D-Day* now refers to 6 June 1944.

**democracy**
A political system in which people vote to elect leaders to govern their country. Equality and freedom are important in a democracy.

**destroyer**
A small, fast warship that attacks enemy ships with weapons such as guns, torpedoes, and depth charges.

**dictator**
A person who rules with absolute power and without effective opposition. Even if a dictator is elected, this person usually rules by force.

**dive-bomber**
An aircraft that dives quickly and steeply towards a target to drop its bombs from close up. This strategy makes it hard for those on the ground to hit with anti-aircraft fire.

**dogfight**
A violent air battle between two or more fighter planes.

**dugout**
A pit dug into the ground, where soldiers can take shelter while firing on the enemy.

**empire**
A group of nations ruled by an emperor or other powerful sovereign, or by a government. Britain, France, and other European countries had empires that included colonies in Africa and Asia.

**Fascism**
A system of government that is led by a dictator who has absolute power and believes that this nation or race is superior to others.

**Final Solution**
A Nazi government programme that intended to kill millions of Jews and other "inferior" peoples who were considered to be enemies of Germany.

**foxhole**
A small pit dug by soldiers to provide shelter from enemy fire.

# 2,000 strips of foil can appear to be a B-17 bomber on a radar screen

# Glossary

**Free French**
Members of the organized movement to continue warfare against Germany after France's 1940 defeat in World War II. Led by General Charles de Gaulle, the Free French eventually managed to unify most of the resistance forces in France.

**fuselage**
The main body of an aircraft, which holds crew and cargo and to which the wings and tail are attached.

**gas mask**
Equipment, worn over the face, that is fitted with a filter to clean the air that the wearer breathes. Gas masks are worn as protection from gas attacks.

**Geneva Conventions**
A series of articles that describe how injured soldiers and POWs should be treated. The first convention was introduced in 1864; Japan and the Soviet Union did not sign the 1929 convention.

**genocide**
The systematic murder of many people from the same racial or cultural group.

**ghetto**
A section of some cities, often a highly populated slum area, where Jews were made to live by the Nazis during World War II.

**Great Depression**
The economic crisis that began with the Wall Street Crash in 1929. It spread worldwide and continued through the 1930s.

**grenade**
A small shell, full of explosives, that can be thrown by hand or fired from a rifle or other device.

**hell ship**
A Japanese ship carrying Allied POWs crammed into the holds, with little to eat or drink.

**Hitler Youth**
The organization set up in Germany by Adolf Hitler to educate and train children ages 13–18. There were two separate groups: one that prepared boys to be soldiers, and one that prepared girls to be mothers.

**Holocaust**
The mass murder of millions of Jews and other minority groups by the Nazis in concentration and death camps.

**ideology**
A set of ideas and beliefs that is shared by a nation, a political system, or a group of people.

**incendiary**
A shell, bomb, or grenade that is designed to start fires.

**internment camp**
A camp for civilian prisoners of war. The US government forced about 110,000 Japanese Americans into internment camps during World War II.

**kamikaze**
Relating to a Japanese tactic during World War II in which a pilot deliberately killed himself by flying his explosives-filled aircraft into a target, such as an enemy ship. *Kamikaze* means "divine wind".

**Luftwaffe**
The German air force. *Luftwaffe* means "air weapon".

**marine**
A soldier who is based on a warship but who also fights on land when necessary.

**mine**
An explosive device that is intended to injure or damage a person, tank, or ship. Land mines are hidden on or under the ground. Naval mines float on or just under the surface of the water.

**Morse code**
A way of sending messages using short and long signals, often called dots and dashes. Morse code can be sent as sounds or flashes of light.

**munitions**
Any weaponry used in combat, such as bombs, missiles, and mines, as well as ammunition.

**nationalist**
A person who is devoted to his or her nation and who may believe that it is better off being ruled independently and acting alone. Extreme nationalists may believe that their nation is superior to other nations or groups of people.

**Nazi**
A member of Hitler's National Socialist Party in Germany, which promoted racist, authoritarian ideas. *Nazi* is short, in English, for the German word *Nationalsozialismus*.

**pact**
An agreement or treaty between two or more nations that brings benefits to all sides.

**partisan**
A member of an armed resistance group fighting for and in his or her occupied country.

**Phoney War**
The period at the beginning of World War II, from September 1939 to May 1940, after Britain and France had declared war on Germany. There was almost no fighting on land, but the nations were preparing for combat.

**Polish Home Army**
A resistance movement in Poland that fought against Nazi and Soviet occupation during the war.

**prisoner-of-war**
A person who is captured and held by the enemy during a war. Most POWs are members of the armed forces.

**propaganda**
Information that is distributed to help or mislead people. During wars, governments use propaganda to encourage their citizens or misinform the enemy.

**radar**
A system that sends out pulses of radio waves to locate the positions of objects, such as planes and ships. *Radar* stands for *RAdio Detecting And Ranging*.

**radiation**
A form of energy released by an atomic bomb. Radiation is very harmful to humans.

**rationing**
The act of controlling the amount of food and other basic items that people are allowed when a war has caused shortages. Petrol, certain foods, clothing, and rubber were rationed in the USA during World War II.

**reconnaissance**
The study of an area to gather information about the position and resources of an enemy.

# Gas masks were issued for free in Britain; most Germans had to pay

### Red Army
The Soviet army, formed in February 1918. The army was increased in size in 1933 to combat the threatened danger from Nazi Germany.

### Red Cross
An international organization founded in Switzerland in 1863 to help victims of conflict. It sent 36 million aid parcels during World War II.

### refugee
A person who has to flee his or her home because of persecution or war. Millions of people became refugees during World War II.

### Reich
A German empire. The First Reich was the Holy Roman Empire (800–1806). The Second Reich was the German Empire (1871–1918). Hitler named his regime the Third Reich (1933–45).

### sabotage
The deliberate damaging of equipment or operations in order to hinder an enemy during war.

### shrapnel
The fragments of metal left after an explosion. British children collected pieces of shrapnel from bomb sites as souvenirs.

### siege
An offensive in which troops surround a city so that no people, food, or supplies can get in or out. Sieges can last for months or even years.

### sniper
A skilled shooter who fires on enemy soldiers from a hiding place, sometimes from a long distance away.

### sonar
A system that sends out pulses of sound, then uses the returning echoes to detect and locate objects underwater. *Sonar* stands for *SOund NAvigation Ranging*.

### stalag
A German prisoner-of-war camp. The largest, Stalag VII-A, held 130,000 Allied soldiers.

### swastika
An ancient cross-shaped symbol, adopted as the Nazi Party's symbol in 1920. It became Germany's national emblem in 1935.

### torpedo
A self-propelled underwater missile that explodes when it hits or get close to a target. Torpedoes were the main weapons used by submarines and U-boats.

### Vichy France
The regime in the unoccupied southern part of France, which was allowed to govern itself after the German occupation of northern France in June 1940. Germany took over Vichy France in November 1942.

### war bond
A government-issued savings bond, sold to raise money during a war. People give money to a government to buy bonds and the government promises to pay the money back, with interest, after the war ends.

### Wehrmacht
The armed forces of the German Third Reich from 1935 to 1945.

## The Welbike
This ingenious motorized bike was used on D-Day. It weighed only 34 kg (75 lbs), yet it could carry a paratrooper in full gear. It was designed to fit in a canister that could be dropped by parachute.

# A

# Index

## PHOTOGRAPHY

1: akg-images; 2–3: Getty Images; 4–5 (background): Fotolia; 6: Library of Congress Prints and Photographs Division; 7l: Time & Life Pictures/Getty Images; 7cl: akg-images; 7cr: Getty Images; 7r: akg-images; 8–9: Getty Images; 10–11: Associated Press; 12l: Library of Congress; 12c: Associated Press; 12r: Roger Viollet/Getty Images; 14tl: Bettmann/Corbis/AP Images; 14tr: Pictorial Press Ltd/Alamy; 14bl: IAM/akg/World History Archive; 14br: akg-images/Interfoto; 15tr: BPK, Berlin/Art Resource; 15bl: Associated Press; 15br: Deutsches Bundesarchiv/Wikimedia Commons; 16tl: Associated Press; 16–17: Three Lions/Getty Images; 17tr, 17cl: Associated Press; 17bc: Thomas Reimer, Fotolia; 18–19 (all): Associated Press; 20 (Mussolini, Hitler): Associated Press; 20br: Time & Life Pictures/Getty Images; 21 (Stalin, Roosevelt): Associated Press; 21br: The Print Collector/Alamy; 23 (Hitler): US National Archives and Records Administration; 24–25: Roger Viollet/Getty Images; 26–27 (maps): Shutterstock; 26br, 27bl: Associated Press; 27bc: ITAR-TASS Photo Agency/Alamy; 28l: Time & Life Pictures/Getty Images; 28c: Dave Bartruff/Corbis; 30tl: IAM/akg/World History Archive; 30tr: Time & Life Pictures/Getty Images; 30bl, 30br: Associated Press; 31tr: Getty Images; 31bl: James King-Holmes/Bletchley Park Trust/Photo Researchers, Inc.; 31br, 32bc: Getty Images; 33b: Associated Press; 34–35: Time & Life Pictures/Getty Images; 36tl: Prisma Bildagentur AG/Alamy; 36c, 36bl, 36bc, 36–37: Jose Lasheras; 37tc: Jean Mounicq/Roger-Viollet/The Image Works; 37tr, 37br: Jose Lasheras; 38–39: Pictorial Press Ltd/Alamy; 39tl: Associated Press; 39tr: RIA Novosti/Alamy; 39c: National Firearms Museum; 40–41: RIA Novosti/Alamy; 42tr: Dave Bartruff/Corbis; 42bl: riekephotos/Shutterstock; 42–43: Imagno/Getty; 45: Photodynamx/Dreamstime; 46 (Land Army): Associated Press; 48tr: AF Archive/Alamy; 50cl: Science Source/Getty Images; 50c: United Archives GmbH/Alamy; 50–51 (Enigma): SSPL/Science Museum/Getty Images; 50–51 (ticker tape), 51tr, 51rc: Jose Lasheras; 51br: Wikimedia Commons; 52l: Library of Congress; 52c: Getty Images; 54tl: Library of Congress; 54tr: Editorial/Dreamstime; 54bl: UC Berkeley, Bancroft Library; 54br: akg-images; 55tl: Associated Press; 55tr: US Navy Photograph, National Archives; 55bl, 55br, 56–57: Library of Congress; 57r: National Archives; 58c, 58bl, 58bc, 58br: Stocktrek Images, Inc./Alamy; 58tr: akg-images; 58–59: Corbis; 59tl, 59tr: akg-images; 60–61: Library of Congress; 62bl: Tiono Sudihadi/Dreamstime; 62–63: Bettmann/Corbis; 63tr: Tiono Sudihadi/Dreamstime; 63br: Mary Evans Picture Library/Alamy; 64b: akg-images; 66–67: Getty Images; 67br: Bettmann/Corbis/AP Images; 68–69 (all): Jose Lasheras; 70bl: Wikimedia Commons; 70tc: Hulton Archive/Getty Images; 70tr: Gaius Cornelius/Wikimedia Commons; 70–71: Popperfoto/Getty Images; 71tl: National Archive; 72tr: US Air Force; 74bl: US Navy; 76–77: Associated Press; 78l: National Archives; 78tr: Getty Images; 80tl: akg-images; 80tr: akg-images/ullstein bild; 80br: akg-images; 81tl: Glenn Berg; 81tr: akg-images; 81bl: Library and Archives Canada; 81br, 82tl: Associated Press; 82–83, 83c: National Archives; 83tr: Jose Lasheras; 84tl: ClassicStock.com/SuperStock; 84 (grenade): Mccool/Dreamstime; 84 (mine, rifle): Jose Lasheras; 86cl: British Army; 87t, 87ct, 87cb, 87b: Jose Lasheras; 88c: Glenn Berg; 88br: Getty Images; 89tl: Associated Press; 89 (background): Time & Life Pictures/Getty Images; 90l: Popperfoto/Getty Images; 90c, 90r: akg-images; 92tl, 92tr: National Archives; 92bl: Library of Congress; 92br: akg-images; 93tr: Library of Congress; 93bl: Trinity Mirror/Mirrorpix/Alamy; 93br: Photo Researchers, Inc.; 94–95: Popperfoto/Getty Images; 96–97: Getty Images; 96c: The Print Collector/Alamy; 96tr: Associated Press; 98l: akg-images; 98–99: Getty Images; 99bc, 100–101: akg-images; 101r: National Archives; 104cl: Mishella/Dreamstime; 104bl: Bettmann/Corbis/AP Images; 104cr: Erik1977/Dreamstime; 104br: Bettmann/Corbis/AP Images; 105tl: Georgios Kollidas/iStockphoto; 105tcl: Wikimedia Commons; 105tcr: Associated Press; 105b: ITAR-TASS Photo Agency/Alamy; 108: Jose Lasheras.

## ARTWORK

15tl, 26bl, 33c: Anders Lejczak; 28r, 31tl, 32c, 48–49, 52r, 72–73, 78c, 84–85, 93tl: Tim Loughhead; all other artwork: Scholastic.

## COVER

Front cover: Popperfoto/Getty Images. Back cover: (tr) Tim Loughhead; (computer monitor) Manaemedia/Dreamstime.

Key to symbols in **More here** columns

*Keywords for web searches*

*Suggested reading*

*Watch on TV, on DVD, or online*

*Listen to songs or recordings*

*Visit exciting places*

*Great things to do*

*Mini-glossary*

# Credits and acknowledgments